奇文共欣赏,疑义相与析。
　　　　　　　——陶渊明

Wonderful essays we cheerfully admire;
With the doubtful points modestly share.
　　　　　　　——Tao Yuanming

《中国传统文化名段名句荟萃·先秦卷》
（英汉对照）

主　编　孙俊芳　郭先英
副主编　李晓婧　李　蕊

河南大学出版社
·郑州·

图书在版编目（CIP）数据

中国传统文化名段名句荟萃. 先秦卷：英汉对照 / 孙俊芳，郭先英主编. —郑州：河南大学出版社，2015.8

ISBN 978-7-5649-2141-5

Ⅰ. ①中… Ⅱ. ①孙… ②郭… Ⅲ. ①英语—汉语—对照读物 ②名句—汇编—中国—先秦时代 Ⅳ. ①H319.4: H

中国版本图书馆CIP数据核字（2015）第210510号

责任编辑　刘利晓
责任校对　范　昕
封面设计　陈盛杰

出版发行	河南大学出版社
	地址　郑州市郑东新区商务外环中华大厦2401号
	邮编：450046
	电话：0371-86059712（高等教育出版分社）
	0371-86059715（营销部）
	网址：www.hupress.com
排　版	郑州市今日文教印制有限公司
印　刷	河南安泰彩印有限公司
版　次	2015年9月第1版　　印　次　2015年9月第1次印刷
开　本	787mm×1092mm　1/16　　印　张　10
字　数	207千字
定　价	25.00元

（本书如有印装质量问题，请与河南大学出版社营销部联系调换）

自　序

在每一种文化的丛林中，总有那么几棵参天大树，它们的枝叶最繁茂，根系最发达，对该民族文化的影响也最深刻，人们称之为经典之作。

什么是经典？为什么要读经典？意大利伊塔洛·卡尔维诺在《为什么读经典》一书中为经典下了这样的定义：

经典是那些你经常听人家说"我正在重读……"而不是"我正在读……"的书。

经典作品是一些产生某种特殊影响的书，它们要么自己以难忘的方式给我们的想象力打下印记，要么乔装成个人或集体的无意识隐藏在深层记忆中。

一部经典作品是一本每次重读都像初读那样带来发现的书。

一部经典作品是一本即使我们初读也好像是在重温的书。

一部经典作品是一本永不会耗尽它要向读者说的一切东西的书。

经典作品是这样一些书，它们带着先前解释的气息走向我们，背后拖着它们经过文化或多种文化（或只是多种语言和风俗）时留下的足迹。

经典作品是这样一些书，我们越是道听途说，以为我们懂了，当我们实际读它们，我们就越是觉得它们独特、意想不到和新颖。

"你的"经典作品是这样一本书，它使你不能对它保持不闻不问，它帮助你在与它的关系中甚至在反对它的过程中确立你自己。①

中国传统文化中无疑有很多这样的经典之作：一咏三叹的《诗经》，荡气回肠的楚辞，风格迥异的唐诗、宋词、元散曲……徜徉在这些经典的作品中，仿佛荡舟于一条文化的河流，两岸落英缤纷，异彩纷呈，风光无限。古希腊教育家、雄辩家伊索克拉底说："独不见蜜蜂乎，无花不采，吮英咀华。博雅之士亦然，滋味遍尝，取精而用弘。"②

而现代快节奏的生活使得快餐文化、网络读物充斥着人们的生活，占据了人们的大部分闲暇时间，手机渐渐异化为人体的一个器官，经典阅读似乎成为尘封的记忆。对博雅的向往使我们一次次拿起久违的经典，然而，紧张的日程安排和急功近利的心态又迫使我们一次次放下。

---

① [意]伊塔洛·卡尔维诺.为什么读经典.黄灿然，李桂蜜译.译林出版社，2012:1~7.

② 钱钟书.管锥编.中华书局，1979:1251.

博大精深的中国古代文化，常让那些有志于做博雅之士的人们慨叹"吾生也有涯，吾知也无涯"。三坟五典、八索九丘、四书五经、百家之言、诗词散曲，这些锦绣般的文字，我们虽然心向往之，却终不能至。于是此书为你提供了一个窗口，可以让你略略品读百家风范，体味诸子思想，群书概要。哲学、文学、医学、艺术、历史、宗教、伦理，时而诗词歌赋，时而雄辩滔滔，如此多的研究领域，如此浩瀚的文化集锦，虽没有通读原著的酣畅淋漓，盛景尽寻，风光遍览，却能让你在有限的时间里"吮英咀华"、"滋味遍尝"。

本书的重要特点在于不仅仅提供了古代文化典籍的精粹和集锦，而且提供了这些名段名句的英语译文，使得对汉学感兴趣的国外读者也可以领略中国文化的魅力。正如迈尔斯·史密斯博士在 KJV《圣经》（钦定版《圣经》）序言中所说的，翻译是打开窗户，让阳光洒进来；敲开坚果的硬壳，使我们尝到果仁；拉开帷幔，使我们得以窥见至圣所；掀开井盖，使我们喝到甘甜的井水……

北京师范大学著名的教育专家肖川博士说："如果一个人从来没有感受过人性光辉的沐浴，从来没有走进过一个丰富而美好的精神世界；如果从来没有读到过一本令他（她）激动不已、百读不厌的读物，从来没有苦苦地思索过某一个问题；如果从来没有一个令他（她）乐此不疲、废寝忘食的活动领域，从来没有过一次刻骨铭心的经历和体验；如果从来没有对自然界的多样与和谐产生过深深的敬畏，从来没有对人类创造的灿烂文化发出过由衷的赞叹……那么，他（她）就没有受到过真正的、良好的教育。"①

让我们一起走进这本读物，一起为中华民族创造的灿烂文化发出由衷的赞叹。

孙俊芳

2015 年 6 月

---

① 肖川.什么是良好的教育.基础教育课程，2014（18）.

Author's Preface

In each cultural forest, there would be some towering trees, with the most luxuriant branches and the deepest roots. These trees are also the most influential in the nation and culture. Thus they are normally called classics.

Then what is a classic? Why should we read classic works? The Italian writer Italo Calvino defines classics in his famous book *Why Should We Read Classics* in this way:

A classic is the book that you often hear people say, "I am re-reading..." instead of "I am reading...".

Classics refer to the books which exert special influence. They either mark our imagination in an unforgettable way, or hide in our deep memory disguised in individual or collective unconsciousness.

A classic is a book that we discover as much in re-reading as in the first reading.

A classic is a book that we feel we are re-reading it even when it's the first reading.

A classic is a book that never exhausts what it is going to tell the readers.

Classics are the books that come up to us with the smell of previous interpretation, leaving behind them the footprints after experiencing various cultures(or maybe only languages and customs).

Classics are the books that the more we hear about them and believe we understand them, the more we feel they are unique, surprising and novel while we practically read them.

"Your" classic is the book that you can't keep ignoring it and it helps you to identify you in the process of your interacting with it or even in your objection to it.

Undoubtedly there are quite a few classics in Chinese traditional culture: the beautifully chanted *The Book of Poetry*, the breathtaking the songs of Chu, and the Tang poetry, Song Ci and Yuan lyrics with various styles. Indulging in reading the classics is like drifting on the river of culture, with both banks covered with beautiful petals showing enchanting scenery. Isocrates, an ancient Greek rhetorician once said, "Just as we see the bee settling on all the flowers, and sipping the best from each, so also those who aspire to culture ought not to leave anything untasted, but should gather useful knowledge from every source."

The fast pace of modern society has filled people's lives with fast-food culture and online reading materials, occupying most of their free time. In an era when the mobile phone is gradually turned into one of our organs, classic reading seems to gradually become old memory covered in dirt. The aspiration to Liberal Learning brings us again and again to the dusty classics on the shelf, but the tight schedule of modern life and the anxiety and eagerness to success force us to put down the books time by time.

The Chinese classics are so extensive and profound, making people who want to be learned and liberal sigh in vain: life is short, but the art is long. All these classic books written in remote antiquity, all the tales, memoirs, poetry and arguments from different schools of academy give us yearning hearts, yet seem so hard to approach. Thus this book opens a window in front of you, through which you can have a bite of different styles of the great minds, and taste the brilliant thoughts and synopses of those classic works. Though not as thoroughly and fully joyful and pleasant as reading the original, the extensive collection from different fields including philosophy, literature, medicine, art, history, religion, and ethics, in either poetic forms or eloquent arguments, enables us to "sip the best from each" and "leave nothing untasted" in limited time.

Another highlight is that this book not only is a collection of the classic sentences and paragraphs, but also provides the English translation of them so that readers from other cultures can have a chance to enjoy the charm of traditional Chinese culture. Just as Dr. Myles Smith put it in the preface of *KJV Bible*, "Translation it is that openeth the window, to let in the light; that breaketh the shell, that we may eat the kernel; that putteth aside the curtain, that we may look into the most holy place; that removeth the cover of the well, that we may come by the water…" [1]

Xiao Chuan, the famous educationist in Beijing Normal University, once said, "A person can't be called well-educated if he / she has never been bathed in the shining glory of human nature, never entered a rich and beautiful spiritual realm, never tirelessly read an inspiring book, never racked his / her brains pondering over a certain question; or has never so indulged in a certain domain that forgotten everything else, has never experienced a unforgettable

---

[1] Myles Smith. *The Translators to the Reader: Holy Bible*. London: Trinitarian Bible Society, 2007: ix.

adventure, has never been awed by the variety and harmony of the nature, has never been amazed by the brilliant culture created by human beings…"

Let's come to this little book, and be amazed at the brilliant culture created by Chinese nation.

Sun Junfang
2015.6

目 录
Contents

《诗经》The Book of Poetry ································· 1

《黄帝内经》Yellow Emperor's Canon of Medicine ············· 13

　《素问》Plain Conversation ······························ 14

　《灵枢》Spiritual Pivot ································· 20

《道德经》Tao Te Ching ····································· 26

《管子》Guanzi ·· 50

《论语》The Analects of Confucius ·························· 62

《墨子》Mozi ·· 78

《孟子》Mencius ··· 88

《庄子》Zhuangzi ·· 99

《荀子》Xunzi ·· 122

《吕氏春秋》The Spring and Autumn of Lü Buwei ············· 136

参考文献 Bibliography ····································· 144

后　记 ··· 145

Epilogue ··· 146

《诗经》
The Book of Poetry

【简介】《诗经》,又称《诗三百》,是我国第一部诗歌总集,收集了自西周初年至春秋时期五百多年的305篇诗歌,分为"风""雅""颂"。其中"风"有十五国风,共160首,汇集了各地的民歌,文学成就最高;"雅"主要是朝廷乐歌,分为"大雅"和"小雅",共105首;"颂"主要是宗庙祭祀之诗歌,共40首。先秦诸子中引用《诗经》者颇多,它被儒家奉为经典。孔子评价《诗经》说:"《诗》三百,一言以蔽之,曰'思无邪'。"[①]

【Introduction】 *The Book of Poetry*, also named *The Book of Three Hundred of Poems*, is the first anthology of poems in China during the five hundred years from the early Western Zhou dynasty (c.1046~771 BC) to the Spring and Autumn period(c.770~476 BC). It is composed of three parts: Feng, Ya, Song. In Feng, 160 poems which are folk songs from fifteen nations enjoy the highest honor in literature. In Ya, 105 poems are divided into the Grater Odes of the Kingdom and the Minor Odes of the Kingdom. In Song, there are 40 poems which are odes of the temple and altar. The sages and scholars before Qin dynasty(c.221~206 BC) frequently quoted the lines in *The Book of Poetry* and regarded it as a Confucian classic. Confucius appraised, "*The Book of Poetry* are three hundred in number. They can be summed up as a word—'pureness'. "

1. 【原文】关关雎鸠,在河之洲;窈窕淑女,君子好逑。　　　　《诗经·国风·关雎》

    【今译】关关鸣叫着的雎鸠,峙立在河中的小洲。高贵娴雅的姑娘啊,真是君子的好配偶。

    【英译】The waterfowl would coo
    　　　　Upon an islet in the brook.
    　　　　A lad would like to woo
    　　　　A lass with nice and pretty look.

2. 【原文】窈窕淑女,寤寐求之。　　　　　　　　　　　　　　《诗经·国风·关雎》

---

① [春秋]孔丘. 论语选萃. 付雅丽译. 中国对外翻译出版公司,2010: 9.

【今译】高贵娴雅的姑娘啊，梦中也在把她追求。

【英译】There lives the pretty lass,

For whom the lad is sick.

3.【原文】窈窕淑女，琴瑟友之。　　　　　　　　　　　　　　　　《诗经·国风·关雎》

【今译】高贵娴雅的姑娘啊，美妙的琴声才让她动情。

【英译】There lives the pretty lass

Whom the lad pursues.

4.【原文】窈窕淑女，钟鼓乐之。　　　　　　　　　　　　　　　　《诗经·国风·关雎》

【今译】高贵娴雅的姑娘啊，快乐的钟鼓为她齐鸣！

【英译】There lives the pretty lass

The lad would entertain.

5.【原文】桃之夭夭，灼灼其华。之子于归，宜其室家。　　　　　　《诗经·国风·桃夭》

【今译】妩媚婀娜的桃树、耀眼的鲜花惹人频顾。这美丽的姑娘今日出嫁，娶亲的人家将和睦幸福。

【英译】The peach tree stands wayside,

With blossoms glowing pink.

I wish the pretty bride

Affluence in food and drink.

6.【原文】南有乔木，不可休息。汉有游女，不可求思。汉之广矣，不可泳思。江之永矣，不可方思。　　　　　　　　　　　　　　　　　　　　　　　　《诗经·国风·汉广》

【今译】南方有挺拔的大树，却无法在树下乘凉。水边那位游玩的姑娘，没法娶她做我的新娘。眼前的汉水浪滔滔啊，没法游过去跟她商量。更有那长江水悠悠啊，想乘筏过去也是妄想！

【英译】The tree in the south is tall,

But does not shade us all;

The maid by the Han is fair,

But brings young men despair.

The Han is much too wide

To swim from side to side.

The Yangtze is too long

To sail the boat along.

7.【原文】维鹊有巢，维鸠居之。之子于归，百两御之。　　　　　　《诗经·国风·鹊巢》

【今译】喜鹊有坚固的鸟巢，布谷鸟前来安家。这姑娘今天出嫁，百辆车子前来迎她。

【英译】When magpies build a nest,
　　　　The cuckoos come to abide.
　　　　Indeed, the bride is blest,
　　　　So many carts await the bride.

8.【原文】未见君子，忧心忡忡。　　　　　　　　　　　　　　《诗经·国风·草虫》

【今译】长久不见我心爱的郎君，一天又一天我忧心不宁。

【英译】As my dear one is not there,
　　　　I'm full of strain and care.

9.【原文】嘒彼小星，三五在东。　　　　　　　　　　　　　　《诗经·国风·小星》

【今译】黎明前闪着微光的残星，三三五五在东方的夜空。

【英译】Little stars are winkling,
　　　　In the east sparsely twinkling.

10.【原文】嘒彼小星，维参与昴。　　　　　　　　　　　　　《诗经·国风·小星》

【今译】黎明前闪着微光的残星，原来是参和昴挂在东方的夜空。

【英译】Little stars are twinkling;
　　　　Star-clusters are winkling.

11.【原文】白茅纯束，有女如玉。　　　　　　　　　　　　《诗经·国风·野有死麕》

【今译】用白茅细心地把它捆好，献给玉一样美丽的姑娘。

【英译】The lass is fair as jade;
　　　　White cogon wreathes her head.

12.【原文】何彼秾矣，华如桃李？平王之孙，齐侯之子。　　《诗经·国风·何彼秾矣》

【今译】是什么繁盛的花如此的艳丽？是那桃红李白锦绣般的美丽。平王之孙容貌娇艳，齐侯之子风度翩翩。

【英译】Why so pretentious is the carriage?
　　　　Its pretty curtains lend the image.
　　　　The king's grand-daughter is to wed
　　　　The son of Marquis Qi, it's said.

13.【原文】耿耿不寐，如有隐忧。微我无酒，以敖以游。　　　《诗经·国风·柏舟》

【今译】我整夜双眸炯炯难以入睡，只因满怀着深深的烦忧。不是我没酒一醉方休，也不是不能遨游散掉忧愁。

【英译】I lie awake all night,
　　　　My heart full of plight.
　　　　To the heavy store of wine,

I do not incline.

14. 【原文】静言思之，不能奋飞。 《诗经·国风·柏舟》

 【今译】让我安静地想想吧又更加烦闷，恨不能展翅飞离这污秽的环境。

 【英译】When I recall all these,

 There can be no release.

15. 【原文】我思古人，俾无訧兮！ 《诗经·国风·绿衣》

 【今译】忘不掉我那去世的爱妻，只有你才使我一生无忧！

 【英译】My memory of her is keen;

 My heart is moved to repine.

16. 【原文】我思古人，实获我心！ 《诗经·国风·绿衣》

 【今译】想起我那过世的爱妻，只有你懂得我的衷肠！

 【英译】My thought is full of remorse;

 In my heart she has a place.

17. 【原文】燕燕于飞，差池其羽。之子于归，远送于野。瞻望弗及，泣涕如雨。

 《诗经·国风·燕燕》

 【今译】燕子在空中自由地飞翔，剪刀似的尾翼临空舒张。今天我妹妹要远嫁他乡，送她到郊外的路旁。眼望她渐渐消失的身影，我的眼泪像雨一样流淌。

 【英译】Two swallows soar to the sky,

 Spreading their wings while they fly.

 My sister is going away;

 I send her on her way.

 When in the distance she disappears,

 My eyes are filled with tears.

18. 【原文】日居月诸，照临下土。 《诗经·国风·日月》

 【今译】太阳啊，月亮啊，光明照彻大地。

 【英译】The sun and the moon divine,

 O'er all the world they shine.

19. 【原文】莫往莫来，悠悠我思。 《诗经·国风·终风》

 【今译】现在你我断绝了交往，这让我整日愁思满怀。

 【英译】He does not come by cart,

 But lingers in my heart.

20. 【原文】死生契阔，与子成说。执子之手，与子偕老。 《诗经·国风·击鼓》

 【今译】"生死离合我永不变心"，这话我们当初已经约定。我也曾紧握着你的双手，

"我跟你走完今生的路程"。

【英译】My wife's my life companion,
We're bound in marital union.
I grasped her hand and say,
"Together we will always stay."

21.【原文】式微，式微，胡不归？微君之故，胡为乎中露？ 《诗经·国风·式微》

【今译】"天黑了，已经黑啦，你为什么还不回家？""要不是为了陪着你，何必泡在这露水里？"

【英译】A wretched state!
Where's our lord?
But for his sake,
Who'd stay abroad?

22.【原文】我思肥泉，兹之永叹。思须与漕，我心悠悠。驾言出游，以写我忧。

《诗经·国风·泉水》

【今译】一想到肥泉流归淇水，我的长叹就有增无休。再想起那须城和漕邑，我的忧伤就更没有尽头。驾着马车我出去遛遛，也许能排遣我的忧愁。

【英译】At the thought of Feiquan Spring,
Memory stirs me to sigh.
When Xu and Cao to mind I bring,
On wings of fancy I fly.
I'd better have a walk—not think!
Some calm my thoughts will clarify.

23.【原文】出自北门，忧心殷殷。 《诗经·国风·北门》

【今译】出了北门我阵阵发冷，满怀的忧愁如此沉重。

【英译】When I leave the Northern Gate,
My grief returns anew.

24.【原文】北风其凉，雨雪其雱。惠而好我，携手同行。其虚其邪？既亟只且！

《诗经·国风·北风》

【今译】那北风是多么寒冷，大雪漫天心已寒透。只有你是那样爱我，我们携手一同出走。岂能再慢慢地等待？我一刻也不能忍受！

【英译】Cold blows the northern wind;
Thick falls the rain and snow.
My family dear, my kin,

Let's take the way and go.

Can't you make up your mind?

There's no time to be slow!

25. 【原文】静女其姝，俟我于城隅。爱而不见，搔首踟蹰。　　《诗经·国风·静女》

【今译】幽静的姑娘多么美丽可爱，她在城上角楼里等我到来。她藏在什么地方我看不见，急得我挠头抓耳四处徘徊。

【英译】A maiden quiet and fair

Awaits me by the Gate.

She hides herself somewhere;

I fidget while I wait.

26. 【原文】鱼网之设，鸿则离之。燕婉之求，得此戚施。　　《诗经·国风·新台》

【今译】我布好了渔网准备网鱼，没想到一只鸿雁网中游。本想找个温厚文雅的公子，得到的却是个驼背老头。

【英译】The net is set for fish,

A toad is caught instead.

A lovely mate she'd wish,

Yet her man's a vicious toad.

27. 【原文】二子乘舟，泛泛其景。愿言思子，中心养养！　　《诗经·国风·二子乘舟》

【今译】两位朋友乘着孤舟，那帆影向远处漂流。这思念如此的沉重，我心中充满了忧愁！

【英译】Two youths drift in a boat

Along the river they float.

My thoughts with them drift there;

My heart is filled with care.

28. 【原文】鬒发如云，不屑髢也。　　《诗经·国风·君子偕老》

【今译】稠密乌黑的头发像乌云，她根本不屑用假发装点。[121]

【英译】Dark and thick is her hair;

No wig she needs to wear.

29. 【原文】人之无良，我以为兄！　　《诗经·国风·鹑之奔奔》

【今译】这个人没有一点良心，凭什么当作兄长称他！

【英译】A man as driven by vice as he,

Alas, my brother he must be,

30. 【原文】相鼠有皮，人而无仪！人而无仪，不死何为？　　《诗经·国风·相鼠》

【今译】那地里的黄鼠还有毛皮,这个人却不讲一点礼仪!一个人要是不讲一点礼仪,他为什么还不死去?

【英译】E'en mice have skin of their own,
But men may be thick-skinned.
If men should be thick-skinned,
Why don't they die alone?

31. 【原文】有匪君子,如切如磋,如琢如磨。　　　　　《诗经·国风·淇奥》

【今译】那位文采风流的君子,就像那切磋过的象牙,就像那琢磨过的美玉。

【英译】My lord is elegant and wise,
As smooth as ivory neatly made,
As carefully polished as a jade.

32. 【原文】手如柔荑,肤如凝脂。　　　　　　　　　　《诗经·国风·硕人》

【今译】她那柔嫩的手就像初生的茅荑,洁白润滑的皮肤像凝脂般白皙。

【英译】Her hands are small, her fingers slim;
Her skin is smooth as cream.

33. 【原文】巧笑倩兮,美目盼兮。　　　　　　　　　　《诗经·国风·硕人》

【今译】妩媚的笑颜是那样灿烂,传情的眼睛清澈又明丽。

【英译】Complement her dimpled cheeks.
And make her black eyes glow.

34. 【原文】夙兴夜寐,靡有朝矣。　　　　　　　　　　《诗经·国风·氓》

【今译】早起晚睡我受了多少辛苦,你想想哪一天我不是这样。

【英译】I start to work at dawn
Until at night I lie down.

35. 【原文】总角之宴,言笑晏晏,信誓旦旦,不思其反。　　《诗经·国风·氓》

【今译】想从小一起快乐的日子,那时有说有笑多么欣欢。我们也明明白白发过誓,没想到如今会违反誓言。

【英译】The happy days are past,
But in memory always last.
I still recall his vow,
Which he abandons now.

36. 【原文】谁谓河广?一苇杭之。　　　　　　　　　　《诗经·国风·河广》

【今译】谁说河水宽广?一只苇筏就能渡过。

【英译】Who says the river is so wide?

A reed boat can drift across the tide.

37. 【原文】投我以木桃，报之以琼瑶。 　　　　　　　　《诗经·国风·木瓜》

   【今译】她赠送我一枚木桃，我回报她一块琼瑶。

   【英译】For a peach thou givest to me,
   　　　　I have a jade for thee.

38. 【原文】知我者，谓我心忧；不知我者，谓我何求。悠悠苍天，此何人哉？
   　　　　　　　　　　　　　　　　　　　　　　　　《诗经·国风·黍离》

   【今译】知道我的人，会说我满腔的忧郁难熬；不知道我的人，会问我为什么这般烦恼。我叩问茫茫无际的苍天，我为什么活得这么糟糕？

   【英译】Those who know my mind
   　　　　Say that I am sad at heart;
   　　　　They fail to know my mind
   　　　　Who say I strain my heart.
   　　　　Gracious Heavens. Oh!
   　　　　Who's brought all this woe?

39. 【原文】君子于役，不知其期。曷至哉？ 　　　《诗经·国风·君子于役》

   【今译】我的丈夫服役去了远方，不知什么时候是个期限，也不知他此刻身在何方？

   【英译】My husband serves the king,
   　　　　No word to me to bring
   　　　　When he'll be home coming.

40. 【原文】扬之水，不流束薪。 　　　　　　　　　《诗经·国风·扬之水》

   【今译】激扬的流水泛着浅浅的波，漂不走小小的一捆柴火。

   【英译】The river waters that surge and spray
   　　　　Can't carry bundled wood away.

41. 【原文】条其啸矣，遇人之不淑矣！ 　　　　《诗经·国风·中谷有蓷》

   【今译】她发出长长的哀伤的叹息，嫁个不合适的人真痛苦。

   【英译】She bitterly sobs and sighs:
   　　　　No good spouse is nigh.

42. 【原文】彼采萧兮，一日不见，如三秋兮！ 　　　　《诗经·国风·采葛》

   【今译】那采香蒿的姑娘，我一天看不见她，就像隔了三年一样！

   【英译】Thou art gathering mugwort there;
   　　　　A day without my seeing thee
   　　　　Seems at least three falls to me.

43. 【原文】父母之言，亦可畏也。　　　　　　　　　　《诗经·国风·将仲子》
    【今译】可是父母那责骂的话，你知道该有多可怕。
    【英译】But what my family say
    　　　　Will worry me all day.

44. 【原文】不如叔也。洵美且仁。　　　　　　　　　　《诗经·国风·叔于田》
    【今译】什么人都不能跟他比。他确实是英俊又温良。
    【英译】My brother betters everyone,
    　　　　So gentle-minded, so handsome.

45. 【原文】子兴视夜，明星有烂。将翱将翔，弋凫与雁。　《诗经·国风·女曰鸡鸣》
    【今译】你起来去看看夜色，启明星是那么灿烂。那水鸟就要起飞了，该为彩礼射只大雁。
    【英译】Rise, Sir, and watch the night,
    　　　　The morning star is shining bright.
    　　　　I'll go out on a chase,
    　　　　To shoot wild ducks and geese.

46. 【原文】琴瑟在御，莫不静好。　　　　　　　　　　《诗经·国风·女曰鸡鸣》
    【今译】我们的生活像弹奏琴瑟，和谐美满，事事称心。
    【英译】In peace and love we'll stay,
    　　　　Ever happy, ever gay.

47. 【原文】有女同车，颜如舜华。将翱将翔，佩玉琼琚。彼美孟姜，洵美且都。
    　　　　　　　　　　　　　　　　　　　　　　　　《诗经·国风·有女同车》
    【今译】这姑娘跟我同坐一辆车上，容貌就像鲜艳的木槿花一样。轻盈的体态有如飞鸟翱翔，她那珍贵的佩玉泛着动人的光彩。她就是美丽的姜家小姐，她真正是美丽娴雅又大方。
    【英译】I'm driving with a maiden fair;
    　　　　Like a blossom is the maid.
    　　　　We roam about from here to there;
    　　　　Brightly shines her gem and jade.
    　　　　Elder Jiang's indeed a beauty rare,
    　　　　With beauty that'll in no case fade.

48. 【原文】风雨凄凄，鸡鸣喈喈。既见君子，云胡不夷！　《诗经·国风·风雨》
    【今译】风疾雨骤寒夜更凄冷，雄鸡啼叫天色将黎明。已经盼回了我的君子，我的心怎么能不平静！

【英译】The storm is bringing chill;

　　　　The cocks are crowing shrill.

　　　　As I have seen my dear,

　　　　How could I keep still.

49.【原文】青青子衿，悠悠我心。　　　　　　　　　　《诗经·国风·子衿》

　【今译】青青的是你送我的佩衿，悠悠的是我想你的苦闷。

　【英译】You wear a collar blue;

　　　　At ease I cannot be.

50.【原文】一日不见，如三月兮。　　　　　　　　　　《诗经·国风·子衿》

　【今译】哪怕是我一天看不到你，就像熬过三月的日程!

　【英译】If you come not one day,

　　　　Three months it seems to be.

51.【原文】出其东门，有女如云。虽则如云，匪我思存。　《诗经·国风·出其东门》

　【今译】我漫步走出都城的东门，眼前的姑娘们密集如云。尽管姑娘们是如此众多，却没有我情怀中的爱人。

　【英译】Off the East Gate is a crowd

　　　　Of fair maids like a colored cloud.

　　　　A colored cloud as they now are,

　　　　They have not moved me so far.

52.【原文】有美一人，清扬婉兮。邂逅相遇，适我愿兮!　《诗经·国风·野有蔓草》

　【今译】夜幕下一个美丽的姑娘，明亮的双眼顾盼多情。无意中我们相会又相爱，真真合了我久盼的心愿!

　【英译】A beauty from afar arises,

　　　　With crescent brows and clear large eyes.

　　　　By chance I meet her on the way,

　　　　Who makes me happy, makes me gay.

53.【原文】鸡既鸣矣，朝既盈矣。　　　　　　　　　　《诗经·国风·鸡鸣》

　【今译】雄鸡叫个不停，太阳也已经东升。

　【英译】The cock has crowed;

　　　　The courtiers leave their abode.

54.【原文】卢令令，其人美且仁。　　　　　　　　　　《诗经·国风·卢令》

　【今译】黑猎犬响着铃声跟着奔走，那个人实在是英俊又温厚。

　【英译】Jingling bells on the neck of his hound,

The hunter is fair and far renowned.

55. 【原文】园有桃，其实之殽。心之忧矣，我歌且谣。不我知者，谓我士也骄。

《诗经·国风·园有桃》

【今译】果园里有一片繁茂的桃树，它的果实足以供我充饥。可是我的心中却忧伤不已，想用歌谣化解满腔的愤激。那些对我一无所知的人们，都说我这个士人傲慢无礼。

【英译】There grows the garden peach,

Its fruits for me to eat.

I'm so sad all along,

Indulged in poem and song.

The strangers used to say,

That I am off the way.

56. 【原文】坎坎伐檀兮，寘之河之干兮。河水清且涟漪。

《诗经·国风·伐檀》

【今译】砍伐檀树山谷里回声叮当，把树干拖到那长长的河岸，河水清清泛起轻微的波纹。

【英译】Chop, chop, we cut the sandalwood,

Piled on the bank raw and crude;

The river ripples in a solemn mood.

57. 【原文】硕鼠硕鼠，无食我黍！三岁贯女，莫我肯顾。逝将去女，适彼乐土。乐土乐土，爰得我所。

《诗经·国风·硕鼠》

【今译】大老鼠啊，大老鼠，不要再吃我的禾黍。为臣这么多年侍奉你，却不肯给我一点照顾。如今我发誓要离开你，去寻找那快乐的疆土。快乐的疆土啊，乐土，哪里才有我立身之处！

【英译】Voles, voles in the field,

Don't eat the crops our labours yield!

Three years now we've let you be,

But never have you thought of me.

I am resolved to leave you,

In the happy land to start anew.

Oh happy land, oh happy land!

Where is the promised land?

58. 【原文】绸缪束薪，三星在天。今夕何夕，见此良人？

《诗经·国风·绸缪》

【今译】紧捆的柴草火炬烧得通亮，夜空中那参星闪烁在东方。今夜究竟是个怎样的夜晚，你见到了这么英俊的新郎？

【英译】Like firewood bundled in wedding ties,

I see the stars of Orion rise.

What special night is this?

My bride's indeed a bliss.

59.【原文】冬之夜，夏之日。 《诗经·国风·葛生》

【今译】冬天的黑夜那么难耐，夏天的白天是那么漫长。

【英译】Night hours in wintertime extend;

Day hours in summer never end.

60.【原文】蒹葭苍苍，白露为霜。所谓伊人，在水一方。溯洄从之，道阻且长。溯游从之，宛在水中央。 《诗经·国风·蒹葭》

【今译】岸边的芦苇一片苍茫，深秋的清晨白露成霜。我辛苦思念的意中人，就在隔水相望的河旁。若逆流而上去接近她，道路那么险阻又漫长。若顺着直流去寻找她，她却好像在那水中央。

【英译】Green reeds are thick and dense;

Clear dews become frost thence.

My love lives far away,

O'er there across the bay.

Seeking her up the streams,

The way is hard and long, I deem.

Seeking her down the streams,

She's in the water, it seems.

61.【原文】彼泽之陂，有蒲与荷。有美一人，伤如之何？寤寐无为，涕泗滂沱！ 《诗经·国风·泽陂》

【今译】在那河对岸的池塘里，长满了清秀的蒲草、荷花。想起那个英俊的小伙儿，除了忧伤能有什么办法？躺下、起来什么也做不成，泪水就像大雨一样泼洒。

【英译】Along the lakeshore by the edge,

Grow the lotus and sweet sedge.

A handsome man is standing there;

How he fills me with despair!

I lie awake by day, by night;

My tears are flooding in a tide.

62.【原文】七月流火，九月授衣。 《诗经·国风·七月》

【今译】七月里火星逐渐向西降，九月里上面分派做衣裳。

【英译】In Month Seven the Fire Star is hardly spotted;
In Month Nine winter coats are allotted.

63.【原文】跻彼公堂，称彼兕觥，万寿无疆。　　　　　　　　《诗经·国风·七月》

【今译】大家齐登国公堂，举起兕角大酒杯，祝一声万寿又无疆。

【英译】Together we go to the lord's hall,
And raise the horn cups above us all,
Wishing a long life to our lord.

《黄帝内经》
Yellow Emperor's Canon of Medicine

【简介】《黄帝内经》分为《素问》和《灵枢》两部分，是我国医学宝库中现存成书最早的一部医学典籍，反映了我国古代医学的辉煌成就，奠定了我国医学发展的基础，是我国劳动人民长期与疾病做斗争的经验总结。人们一般认为它起源于轩辕黄帝，代代口耳相传，成书于春秋战国时期，非一人所著。它以黄帝、岐伯、雷公等人对话、问答的形式论述了人体的生理、病理、诊断、治疗、摄生等问题；以阴阳五行学说为指导，强调了人与自然的密切关系以及人体内部协调统一的整体观念。

【Introduction】 *Yellow Emperor's Canon of Medicine* is composed of two separate books, *Plain Conversation* and *Spiritual Pivot*. It is the earliest extant medical canon in China that records the experience and achievements made by Chinese people in ancient times during the long-term struggle with illness. It is generally believed that it originates from Xuanyuan, Huangdi, and is passed down orally, then compiled in the period of Spring and Autumn and Warring States(c.770~221 BC) by more than one author. Through the conversation between Huangdi and Qibo, Leigong, it describes physiology, pathology, diagnosis, treatment of the human body and health cultivating. Based on the theory of Yin and Yang and Wuxing, it emphasizes the close relationship between human and nature, and harmonic coexistence about the different functions of human body.

《素问》

Plain Conversation

1. 【原文】上古之人，其知道者，法于阴阳，和于术数，食饮有节，起居有常，不妄作劳，故能形与神俱，而尽终其天年，度百岁乃去。　　　　　　　　《素问·上古天真论篇第一》

   【今译】上古时的人，懂得养生之道，他们遵循阴阳变化的规律，掌握养生的方法，饮食有节制，起居有规律，不过分劳累，所以他们能形神俱旺，颐养天年，活到百岁后才离开人世。

   【英译】The sages in ancient times who knew the Tao(the tenets for cultivating health) followed the rules of Yin and Yang and adjusted Shushu(the ways to cultivate health). They were moderate in eating and drinking, regular in working and resting, avoiding any overstrain. That is why they could maintain a desirable harmony between the Shen(mind or spirit) and the body, enjoying good health and a long life.

2. 【原文】夫上古圣人之教下也，皆谓之虚邪贼风，避之有时，恬淡虚无，真气从之，精神内守，病安从来。是以志闲而少欲，心安而不惧，形劳而不倦，气从以顺，各从其欲，皆得所愿。故美其食，任其服，乐其俗，高下不相慕，其民故曰朴。是以嗜欲不能劳其目，淫邪不能惑其心。　　　　　　　　　　《素问·上古天真论篇第一》

   【今译】上古时圣人教导百姓的时候，总是强调要适时地避开四时不正之气，思想上要清净安闲，消除杂念，保持真气调畅，精神守持于内。这样，疾病怎么能发生呢？他们精神安闲，少有欲望，心境平和，没有焦虑。他们虽然劳作，但不过度疲劳，真气因而调顺，各人的愿望都能得以满足。所以他们吃什么食物都觉得甘美，穿什么衣服都感到舒服。他们满意于自己的风俗习惯，不美慕彼此之间地位的高低，生活得朴实自然。正因为如此，不当嗜好不能扰乱他们的视听，淫邪之举不能惑乱他们的心境。

   【英译】When the sages in ancient times taught the people, they emphasized the importance of avoiding Xuxie(Deficiency-Evil) and Zeifeng(Thief-Wind) in good time and keep the mind free from avarice. In this way Zhenqi in the body will be in harmony, Jingshen(Essence-Spirit) will remain inside, and diseases will have no way to occur. Therefore people in ancient times all lived in peace and contentment, without any fear. They worked, but never overstrained themselves, marking it smooth for Qi to flow. They all felt satisfied with their lives and enjoyed their tasty food, natural clothes and naive customs. They did not desire for high positions and lived simply and naturally. That was why improper addiction and avarice could not distract their eyes and ears, obscenity and fallacy could not tempt their mind.

3. 【原文】外不劳形于事，内无思想之患，以恬愉为务，以自得为功。

《素问·上古天真论篇第一》

【今译】在外不使形体因事物而劳累，在内无思想负担，以安静、愉快为目的，以悠然自得为满足。

【英译】Physically, they tried not to exhaust their bodies; mentally, they freed themselves from any anxiety, regarding peace and happiness as the target of their lives, and taking self-contentment as the symbol of achievement.

4. 【原文】有贤人者，法则天地，象似日月，辨列星辰，逆从阴阳，分别四时，将从上古，合同于道，亦可使益寿而有极时。

《素问·上古天真论篇第一》

【今译】还有被称为"贤人"的人，他们能根据天地的变化规律、日月的升降现象，辨明星辰排列的位置，顺从阴阳的消长，适应四时的变化，顺从上古真人的养生之道，也能延年益寿，但有终极之时。

【英译】The virtuous people who abode by the laws of the earth and the heaven, imitated the changes of the sun and the moon, followed the varying order of the stars, adhered to the changes of Yin and Yang, differentiated the four seasons, and acted in accordance with the practice of the immortal beings in ancient times. In this way they prolonged their lives.

5. 【原文】从阴阳则生，逆之则死，从之则治，逆之则乱。《素问·四气调神大论篇第二》

【今译】顺应阴阳的消长变化，就能生存，违逆了就会死亡。顺从了阴阳的变化，就会正常；违逆了，就会引起紊乱。

【英译】Following the rules of Yin and Yang ensures life while violating them leads to death. Abidance by them brings about peace while violation of them results in disorders.

6. 【原文】是故圣人不治已病治未病，不治已乱治未乱，此之谓也。

《素问·四气调神大论篇第二》

【今译】所以圣人不是等到疾病已经发生再去治疗，而是在疾病发生之前就进行预防；不是等到乱子已经发生再去治理，而是在它发生之前就采取防治措施，其道理就在这里。

【英译】Therefore, the sages usually pay less attention to the treatment of a disease, but more to the prevention of it. Also, they usually pay less attention to the solution of a trouble, but more to the prevention of it.

（李晓婧改译）

7. 【原文】夫精者，身之本也。　　　　　　　　　　　　《素问·金匮真言论篇第四》

【今译】精，是人体的根本。

【英译】Jing(Essence) is the foundation of the body.

8. 【原文】阴中有阴，阳中有阳。 《素问·金匮真言论篇第四》

   【今译】阴阳之中，还各有阴阳。

   【英译】That is why it is said that there is Yin within Yin and Yang within Yang.

9. 【原文】非其人勿教，非其真勿授，是谓得道。 《素问·金匮真言论篇第四》

   【今译】对于那些不是有志于医学或者不具备一定条件的人，切勿轻易传授。这才是爱护和珍视这门学问的正确态度。

   【英译】But do not teach these abstruse theories to anyone not eligible or unqualified to study them. This is the right way to pass on such valuable theories.

10. 【原文】阴阳者，天地之道也，万物之纲纪，变化之父母，生杀之本始，神明之府也，治病必求于本。 《素问·阴阳应象大论篇第五》

    【今译】阴阳是自然界的规律，是一切事物的纲纪，是万物变化的根源，是生长、毁灭的根本，是事物各种运动现象的原动力。凡医治疾病，必须求得病情阴阳变化的根本。

    【英译】Yin and Yang serve as the Tao(law) of the heavens and the earth, the fundamental principle of all things, the parents of change, the beginning of birth and death and the storehouse of Shenming. The treatment of disease must follow this law.

11. 【原文】以我知彼，以表知里。 《素问·阴阳应象大论篇第五》

    【今译】通过自己的正常状态来了解病人的异常状态，从外在的症状诊知内在的病变。

    【英译】By comparing the normal conditions of themselves with the abnormal conditions of the patients, they understand the pathological changes of the patients; by examining the manifestations in the exterior, they know the pathological changes in the interior.

12. 【原文】天覆地载，万物方生。 《素问·阴阳离合论篇第六》

    【今译】天地之间，万物初生。

    【英译】The protection of the heaven and the support of the earth give rise to the origination of everything.

13. 【原文】天为阳，地为阴，日为阳，月为阴，行有分纪，周有道理。

    《素问·六节脏象论篇第九》

    【今译】天属阳，地属阴，日属阳，月属阴。它们的运行有一定的区域和秩序，其环周也有一定的轨迹。

    【英译】The heaven pertains to Yang while the earth to Yin. The sun belongs to Yang while the moon to Yin. They move in certain regions according to certain order and along certain orbits.

14. 【原文】心者，生之本，神之处，其华在面，其充在血脉，为阳中之太阳，通于夏气。

《素问·六节脏象论篇第九》

【今译】心，是生命的根本，为神之居处，其荣华表现于面部，其充养在血脉，为阳中之太阳，与夏气相通。

【英译】The heart is the root of life and the house of Shen(Spirit). The heart demonstrates its Hua(Splendor) on the face, nourishing the blood vessels, pertaining to Taiyang within Yang and related to Xiaqi(Summer-Qi).

15. 【原文】故东方之域，天地之所始生也。　　《素问·异法方宜论篇第十二》

【今译】东方地区得天地始生之气。

【英译】The east is the place where all the things in nature start to grow.

16. 【原文】西方者，金玉之域，沙石之处，天地之所收引也。

《素问·异法方宜论篇第十二》

【今译】西方地区，盛产金玉，遍地沙石，其地有秋季收敛引急的气象。

【英译】The west, rich in metal, sand and stones, is the place marked by astringency in nature.

17. 【原文】北方者，天地所闭藏之域也。　　《素问·异法方宜论篇第十二》

【今译】北方地区，为自然界之气闭藏之域。

【英译】The north is a place of closure and storage in nature.

18. 【原文】中央者，其地平以湿，天地所以生万物也众。

【今译】中央之地，地形平坦而潮湿，物产丰富。

【英译】The central region, plain and humid, is the place rich in a variety of products.

19. 【原文】病为本，工为标，标本不得，邪气不服，此之谓也。

《素问·汤液醪醴论篇第十四》

【今译】病人为本，医生为标，病人与医生不能很好合作，病邪就不能制服，道理就是这样。

【英译】Diseases are Ben(Root) and the diagnosis and treatment of doctors are Biao(Branch). If Biao and Ben do not agree with each other, Xieqi(Evil-Qi) cannot be eliminated. That is why diseases cannot be cured.

20. 【原文】万物之外，六合之内，天地之变，阴阳之应，彼春之暖，为夏之暑，彼秋之忿，为冬之怒。

《素问·脉要精微论篇第十七》

【今译】万物之外，六合之内，天地间的变化，阴阳四时与之相应。如春天的温暖发展为夏天的暑热，秋天的劲急发展为冬天的严寒。

【英译】Among all things in nature and within the Liuhe, all changes in heaven and on the earth correspond to the variations of Yin and Yang in the four seasons. For example, the warmth in spring turns into heat in summer, and strong wind in autumn develops into ferocious cold in winter.

21. 【原文】天地之至数，始于一，终于九焉。一者天，二者地，三者人。因而三之，三三者九，以应九野。 　　《素问·三部九候论篇第二十》

【今译】天地的至数，始于一，终于九。一代表天，二代表地，三代表人；天地人合而为三，三三为九，以应九野之数。

【英译】The most important rule of the heaven and the earth starts from number one and ends at number nine. Number one corresponds to the heaven, number two to the earth and number three to human beings. That is what number one, number two and number three stand for. Three times three makes nine which corresponds to the nine administrative regions.

22. 【原文】天覆地载，万物悉备，莫贵于人，人以天地之气生，四时之法成。 　　《素问·宝命全形论篇第二十五》

【今译】天覆于上，地载于下，万物俱备，但万物之中没有比人更宝贵的了。人依靠天地之气而生存，并随着四时规律而生活。

【英译】The covering of the heaven in the upper and the support of the earth in the lower have paved the way for the creation of all things in nature, among which the most noble one is man who exists on the dependence of the Tianqi(Heaven-Qi) and Diqi(Earth-Qi) and lives in accordance with the principle of the four seasons.

23. 【原文】夫人生于地，悬命于天，天地合气，命之曰人。 　　《素问·宝命全形论篇第二十五》

【今译】人成形于地而命赋予天，天地之气相合，才产生了人。

【英译】Man is born on the earth and is endowed with life by the heaven. Owing to the integration of the Tianqi and Diqi, man comes into existence.

24. 【原文】此所谓圣人易语，良马易御也。 　　《素问·气穴论篇第五十八》

【今译】这真是所谓"圣人容易先语，良马容易驾驭"啊！

【英译】This is just what sages are easy to talk with and good horses are easy to ride on means.

25. 【原文】天有五行，御五位，以生寒暑燥湿风；人有五脏，化五气，以生喜怒思忧恐。 　　《素问·天元纪大论篇第六十六》

【今译】天有五行，临治于五位，从而产生寒、暑、燥、湿、风等气候变化。人有五脏，化生五志，从而产生喜、怒、思、忧、恐等情绪变化。

【英译】In nature there exists the Wuxing(Five-Elements) that governs the five directions to produce cold, summer heat, dryness, dampness and wind; in the human body there exist Five Zang-Organs that transform five kind of Qi to generate the emotions of joy, anger, contemplation, anxiety and fear.

26. 【原文】夫五运阴阳者，天地之道也，万物之纲纪，变化之父母，生杀之本始，神明之府也，可不通乎！故物生谓之化，物极谓之变，阴阳不测谓之神，神用无方谓之圣。夫变化之为用也，在天为玄，在人为道，在地为化，化生五味，道生智，玄生神。

《素问·天元纪大论篇第六十六》

【今译】五运和阴阳是自然界的一般规律，是自然万物的总纲，是事物发展变化的基础，是生长毁灭的根本，是宇宙间无穷变化之所在。这些道理怎么能不通晓呢！因而事物的生长叫作化，发展到极点叫作变，难以探测的阴阳变化叫作神，能够掌握和运用这种无穷变化原则的人，叫作圣。阴阳变化的作用，在天则表现为深远无穷，在人则表现为对自然规律的认识，在地则表现为万物的生化。地的生化产生五味，对自然规律的认识产生智慧，在深远的宇宙空间产生了无穷尽的变化。

【英译】The Wuyun(Five-Motions) and Yin and Yang are the Tao(law) of the heaven and earth, the fundamental principle of all things, the parents of change, the beginning of birth and death and the storehouse of Shenming. One must be aware of these tenets. The beginning of things is called Hua(Transformation), the extreme development of things is called Bian(Chang), undetectable changes of Yin and Yang is called Shen and those who can master and control such a Shen is called Sheng(sages). The changes of Yin and Yang demonstrate as Xuan(Profoundness and Mysteriousness) in the heaven, as Tao in human beings and as Hua on the earth. The activity of Hua generates five flavors, the practice of Tao generates wisdom, the permeation of Xuan generates Shen.

27. 【原文】形精之动，犹根本之与枝叶也。仰观其象，虽远可知也。

《素问·五运行大论篇第六十七》

【今译】大地上的物质与天空中的日月五星的运动，就像根本和枝叶的关系。虽然距离很远，但通过仰观其象，仍然可以知道它们的情况。

【英译】The motion of the forms on the earth and the essence in the heaven are just like the root and twigs of a tree. Though located far away, it can be cognized by observation of the images.

28. 【原文】夫物之生从于化，物之极由乎变，变化之相薄，成败之所由也。

《素问·六微旨大论篇第六十八》

【今译】物体生于化，物体发展到了极点就要变，变和化的互相斗争与转化，是成败的根本原因。

【英译】The growth of things depends on Hua while the utmost development of things results from Bian. The struggle between Bian and Hua decides success and failure.

《灵枢》
Spiritual Pivot

1. 【原文】夫气之在脉也，邪气在上，浊气在中，清气在下。 《灵枢·九针十二原第一》

   【今译】邪气侵犯经脉时，多伤人体上部；饮食不节，寒温不适，浊气停于人体中部；清冷寒湿之邪，多伤人体下部。

   【英译】When Qi has invaded the Channels, Xieqi is in the upper, Zhuoqi(Turbid-Qi) is in the middle and Qingqi(Lucid-Qi) is in the lower.

2. 【原文】此四时之序，气之所处，病之所舍，脏之所宜。 《灵枢·本输第二》

   【今译】四时阴阳消长有一定的秩序，人体的气血盛衰也随之变化，疾病的发生也有相应的部位，用针也要与之相宜。

   【英译】These are the needling methods used according to the order of the four seasons, the condition of Qi, the location of diseases and the states of the Zang-Organs.

3. 【原文】愁忧恐惧则伤心，形寒寒饮则伤肺，以其两寒相感，中外皆伤，故气逆而上行。

   《灵枢·邪气脏腑病形第四》

   【今译】愁忧恐惧则伤心，形体受寒或吃寒冷的饮食则伤肺，因为两种寒邪同时感受，表里均受损，所以发生咳喘等肺气上逆的病变。

   【英译】Anxiety, worry and fear will damage the heart. Attack of cold and drinking cold water damage the lung. Mixture of double cold will damage both the external and internal, and therefore making Qi flow adversely upwards.

4. 【原文】天地相感，寒暖相移，阴阳之道，孰少孰多，阴道偶，阳道奇。

   《灵枢·根结第五》

   【今译】天气和地气相互感应，寒暖相互交替推移，阴阳的变化或少或多都是有一定规律的。阴道为偶数，阳道为奇数。

   【英译】The heaven and the earth are interacting on each other. Cold and warmth are alternating with each other. There is a definite rule of Yin and Yang in waning and waxing. The rule of Yin in changing is even in number and the rule of Yang in changing is odd in number.

5. 【原文】调阴与阳，精气乃光，合形与气，使神内藏。　　　　　《灵枢·根结第五》

   【今译】调和阴阳，精气才能充沛，形体与精气相互维系，神气才能内藏不泄。

   【英译】Only when Yin and Yang are regulated can Jingqi(Essence-Qi) be replenished, the body and Qi be integrated and the Spirit be maintained inside.

6. 【原文】余闻人之生也，有刚有柔，有弱有强，有短有长，有阴有阳。

   《灵枢·寿夭刚柔第六》

   【今译】我听说人的禀赋不同，有刚柔强弱之分，有短长阴阳之别。

   【英译】I have heard that the constitution of human being is either sturdy or soft and weak or strong, the body is either short or long, and the physical portions and the pathological changes are either Yin or Yang.

7. 【原文】风寒伤形，忧恐忿怒伤气。气伤脏，乃病脏。　　《灵枢·寿夭刚柔第六》

   【今译】风寒外袭伤人形体，忧恐忿怒内扰影响气机。气机受阻必然伤及脏腑，引起脏腑病变。

   【英译】Wind and cold damage the body while anxiety, fear and anger impair Qi. Impairment of Qi eventually affects the viscera and leads to visceral disorders.

8. 【原文】形与气相任则寿，不相任则夭。皮与肉相果则寿，不相果则夭，血气经络，胜形则寿，不胜形则夭。　　　　　　　　　　　　《灵枢·寿夭刚柔第六》

   【今译】形与气相应则长寿，不相应就夭亡。皮和肉相应就长寿，不相应就夭亡。气血经络胜于形体的就长寿，气血经络不胜于形体的就夭亡。

   【英译】If a person's physique is equivalent to Qi inside his body, he will live a long life; if a person's physique is not equivalent to Qi inside his physique, he will live a short life. If a person's skin and muscles are equivalent to each other, he will live a long life; if a person's skin and muscles are not equivalent to each other, he will live a short life. If a person's blood, Qi, Channels and Collaterals are stronger than the physique, he will live a long life; if a person's blood, Qi, Channels and Collaterals are not stronger than the physique, he will live a short life.

9. 【原文】天之在我者德也，地之在我者气也。德流气薄而生者也。《灵枢·本神第八》

   【今译】天赋予人的是德，地赋予人的是气。天地交感而万物化生。

   【英译】What the heaven has endowed man is called De. What the earth has endowed man is called Qi. The result brought about by the communication between the endowment of the heaven and the endowment of the earth is Sheng(Birth).

10. 【原文】故智者之养生也，必顺四时而适寒暑，和喜怒而安居处，节阴阳而调刚柔。

如是则僻邪不至，长生久视。　　　　　　　　　　　　　《灵枢·本神第八》

【今译】所以有智慧的人养生，必然顺应四时季节寒暖变化，避免情绪激动，生活起居有规律，调节身体的阴阳刚柔，这样就能避免病邪侵袭，从而健康长寿。

【英译】So the sages cultivate their health by means of adapting themselves to cold and heat, balancing joy and anger, maintaining a regular daily life, adjusting Yin and Yang and regulating sturdiness and softness. In such a way, they are able to avoid attack of Xie(Evil) and live a long life.

11.【原文】肝悲哀动中则伤魂。　　　　　　　　　　　　　《灵枢·本神第八》

【今译】肝脏因过分悲哀而伤魂。

【英译】Excessive sorrow and grief in the liver will harm the internal organs and damage the Ethereal Soul.

12.【原文】肺喜乐无极则伤魄。　　　　　　　　　　　　　《灵枢·本神第八》

【今译】肺脏喜乐太过则伤魄。

【英译】Excessive joy and happiness in the lung will damage the Corporeal Soul.

13.【原文】肾盛怒而不止则伤志。　　　　　　　　　　　　　《灵枢·本神第八》

【今译】肾脏过度愤怒就会伤志。

【英译】Excessive rage in the kidney without relief will damage the ability to understand the external world.

14.【原文】恐惧而不解则伤精。　　　　　　　　　　　　　《灵枢·本神第八》

【今译】恐惧不解则伤精。

【英译】Constant fear without relief will damage Essence.

15.【原文】春气在毛，夏气在皮肤，秋气在分肉，冬气在筋骨。　　《灵枢·终始第九》

【今译】春天病邪伤人，多在表浅的皮毛部；夏天病邪伤人，多在浅层的皮肤；秋天病邪伤人，多在分肉部；冬天病邪伤人，多在筋骨部。

【英译】The invasion of pathogenic factors into the body varies in depth in different seasons. In spring, pathogenic factors tend to attack hairs; in summer, pathogenic factors tend to attack skin; in autumn, pathogenic factors tend to attack muscular interstices; and in winter, pathogenic factors tend to attack tendons and bones.

16.【原文】天至高不可度，地至广不可量，此之谓也。且夫人生于天地之间，六合之内，此天之高，地之广也，非人力之所能度量而至也。　　《灵枢·经水第十二》

【今译】天高不可测，地广不可量，这是所谓不易解决的问题。人虽生活在天地之间，六合之内，就像天之高、地之广一样，不是人力所能测量出来的。

【英译】The heaven is so high that its height cannot be measured. The earth is so broad that its width cannot be determined. The reason is just like that. Human beings live between the earth and the heaven and within the six directions. The height of the heaven and the width of the earth are beyond the ability of human beings to measure.

17. 【原文】忧思则心系急，心系急则气道约，约则不利，故太息以伸出之。

《灵枢·口问第二十八》

【今译】忧愁思虑则心系急迫，心系急迫就约束气道，气道约束就呼吸不利，所以不时叹息以伸展其气。

【英译】Worry and contemplation will tighten up the heart system. When the heart system is tightened up, the passageways of Qi will be restricted. When the passageways of Qi are restricted, they will become unsmooth. That is why people are sighing in order to breathe out.

18. 【原文】入国问俗，人家问讳，上堂问礼，临病人问所便。 《灵枢·师传第二十九》

【今译】到达一个国家后，要先问清当地的风俗习惯；进入一个家庭，要先问清人家的忌讳；登堂时要先问清人家的礼节；临症时，要先问清病人的喜好。

【英译】When one wants to enter into another country, he has to get familiar with the customs followed by people in that country; when one wants to go to others' family, he must try to know the taboos held in that family; when one wants to enter into a hall, he has to inquire about the etiquettes; when one is going to treat a patient, he must be clear about the preference of the patient.

19. 【原文】春夏先治其标，后治其本；秋冬先治其本，后治其标。

《灵枢·师传第二十九》

【今译】春夏之季，先治其标，后治其本；秋冬之季，先治其本，后治其标。

【英译】In spring and summer, treatment should concentrate on the Branch first and then on the Root; in autumn and winter, treatment should concentrate on the Root first and then on the Branch.

20. 【原文】食饮者，热无灼灼，寒无沧沧。寒温中适，故气将持，乃不致邪僻也。

《灵枢·师传第二十九》

【今译】饮食也不要过热过冷。寒热适中，正气就能内守，邪气也就无法侵入人体了。

【英译】In terms of food, the patient should avoid eating food that is very hot though it needs to be hot and food that is very cold though it should be cold. In a word, the food taken and the clothes put on must be adjusted according to the change of weather. In this way, Qi(Healthy-Qi) will be maintained inside and Xieqi will have no way to attack the body.

21. 【原文】肝者主为将，使之候外，欲知坚固，视目小大。 《灵枢·师传第二十九》

【今译】肝为将军之官，开窍于目，预知肝脏是否坚固，可以观察眼睛的大小。

【英译】Among the five Zang-Organs and the Six Fu-Organs, the liver acts as a general to protect the external part of the body and opens to the eyes. Whether the liver is solid or not can be determined by inspecting the size of the eyes.

22.【原文】有道以来，有道以去，审知其道，是谓身宝。　　《灵枢·五乱第三十四》

【今译】疾病的发生是有规律的，疾病的治疗也有一定的规律。掌握这种规律，对保持人体功能的正常是十分宝贵的。

【英译】The occurrence of diseases must follow certain rules and so does the healing of diseases. To be aware of these rules is key to the protection of life.

23.【原文】圣人之为道者，上合于天，下合于地，中合于人事，必有明法。

《灵枢·逆顺肥瘦第三十八》

【今译】圣人所认识的事物规律，上合天文，下合地理，中合人事，必定有明确的法度和标准。

【英译】The methods followed by sages in studying conform to the heaven in the upper region, accord with the earth in the lower region and tally with human affairs in the middle region. Hence they do everything in keeping with certain rules and principles.

24.【原文】余闻天为阳，地为阴，日为阳，月为阴。　　《灵枢·阴阳系日月第四十一》

【今译】我听说天为阳，地为阴，日为阳，月为阴。

【英译】I have heard that the heaven is Yang and the earth is Yin; the sun is Yang and the moon is Yin.

25.【原文】病先发于肺，三日而之肝，一日而之脾，五日而之胃，十日不已，死。

《灵枢·病传第四十二》

【今译】若疾病先发生在肺，过三天就传到肝，再过一天就传到脾，再过五天就传到胃，如再过十天不愈，就会死亡。

【英译】If the disease first occurs in the lung, after three days it will be transmitted to the liver, after one day it will be transmitted to the spleen and after five days it will be transmitted to the stomach. If it still cannot be cured after ten more days, death is inevitable.

26.【原文】春生，夏长，秋收，冬藏，是气之常也，人亦应之，以一日分为四时，朝则为春，日中为夏，日入为秋，夜半为冬。　　《灵枢·顺气一日分为四时第四十四》

【今译】春天阳气生发，夏天阳气隆盛，秋天阳气收敛，冬天阳气闭藏，这是一年中四时阳气变化的一般规律，人体的阳气变化也与此相应。以一昼夜来分四时，早晨为春，中午为夏，傍晚为秋，半夜为冬。

【英译】Spring is the season characterized by resuscitation, summer is the season characterized by growth, autumn is the season characterized by harvest and winter is the season characterized by storage. This is the normal changes of Qi to which human body also responds. To divide one day into the four seasons, the morning corresponds to spring, the noon corresponds to summer, evening corresponds to autumn and midnight corresponds to winter.

27.【原文】日与月焉，水与镜焉，鼓与响焉。夫日月之明，不失其影，水镜之察，不失其形，鼓响之应，不后其声，动摇则应和，尽得其情。　　《灵枢·外揣第四十五》

【今译】事物之间有着密切的联系，如同日与月、水与镜和鼓与响一样。日月照耀物体，马上就会有影子出现；水和镜反映事物外貌，从不扭曲其形；击鼓发声，音不迟后。当一种变化出现时，就有一定的反应相随。了解了这个道理，就掌握了用针的理论。

【英译】Things in the natural world are closely related to each other, just like the sun and the moon, water and mirror, drum and sound. When the light of the sun and the moon shines, the shadow of things immediately follows; when the water and mirror are used to examine things, the physical shape of things is clearly reflected; when the drum is beat by a drumstick, the sound immediately follows. This phenomenon shows that the occurrence of a change will be immediately followed by a corresponding response, just like that of shadow, shape and sound. If one has understood this basic rule, he will grasp the gist of the theory of acupuncture.

28.【原文】视其外应，以知其内脏，则知所病矣。　　《灵枢·本脏第四十七》

【今译】观察外在的表现，就可知道脏腑的情况，从而了解脏腑所发生的病变。

【英译】Observation of the external manifestations of the viscera can reveal the states of the viscera inside the body and predict the diseases that may occur in the viscera.

29.【原文】以母为基，以父为楯；失神者死，得神者生也。　　《灵枢·天年第五十四》

【今译】以母之血为基础，以父之精为卫外；丧失神气的就会死亡，有了神气才能维持生命。

【英译】The base of life is the Yin-Blood of the mother; the defense of life is the Yang-Essence of the father. Loss of the Shen which is produced by mixture of the mother's Yin-Blood and the father's Yang-Essence will lead to death and preservation of the Shen inside the body will guarantee life.

《道德经》
Tao Te Ching

【简介】《道德经》又称《老子》，是中国古代先秦诸子分家前的一部著作，是道家哲学思想的重要来源。《道德经》分为上下两篇，原文上篇为《德经》，下篇为《道经》，后改为《道经》在前，《德经》在后，并分为81章，全文共约5 000字。它是中国历史上首部完整的哲学著作，被看作是一部道家的经典。《道德经》传说是春秋时期的老子（公元前600年至前470年左右）所撰写。老子是春秋时期伟大的思想家、道家学派创始人。老子对人类的贡献在于他博大精深的思想。老子思想是中国人揭示自然界奥秘的一种尝试，在中国哲学史上，老子第一个系统地提出了"道"，这个"道"来源于自然，以"无"为本，以"有"为用，以"反始守柔"为处事之方。"反者，道之动；弱者，道之用。天下万物生于有，有生于无"成为《道德经》五千言的纲领。

【Introduction】 *Tao Te Ching*, also called *Lao Tzu*, is a book of the pre-Qin period. It is the important source of the Taoist philosophy. Originally, *Tao Te Ching* consists of two parts, with *Dejing* being the first part and *Daojing* being the second. Later, it is refined into 81 chapters, with *Daojing* ahead of *Dejing*. Comprised of 5 000 characters, *Tao Te Ching* is the first complete philosophical work in Chinese history, and has been hitherto considered a classic of Taoism. It is said that *Tao Te Ching* is written by Lao Tzu(c.600~470 BC). Lao Tzu is one of the greatest thinkers during the Spring and Autumn period, and also the founder of Taoism. The contribution of Lao Tzu to mankind lies in his profound thoughts. Lao Tzu's thoughts represent the attempt of ancient Chinese to unveil nature's mysteries. Lao Tzu is the first philosopher in China to have put forward a "Tao" systematically, which originates in nature, with "Non-being" as its essence, with "Being" as its function, with "returning to the beginning and holding on to what is weak" as the basic policy of conduct. "In Tao the only motion is returning; the only useful quality, weakness. For though all creatures under heaven are the products of Being, Being itself is the product of Non-being" can be taken as the gist of the 5 000 characters of *Tao Te Ching*. Lao Tzu's thoughts have exerted great influence throughout the history of China.

《道德经》
Tao Te Ching

1. 【原文】道可道，非常道；名可名，非常名。无名，天地之始。有名，万物之母。故常无欲，以观其妙。常有欲，以观其徼。此两者同出而异名，同谓之玄。玄之又玄，众妙之门。

《道德经》第一章

【今译】"道"如果可以用言语来清楚表述的，那就不是永恒的"道"；"名"如果可以用名称去明白界定的，那就不是永恒不变的"名"。"无名"（名称未定之前），可以用来表述天地混沌未开的初始状态；"有名"（名称已定以后），则是宇宙万物得以产生的母体本源。因此，总是在欲望消解时，才可以看出起源于无以名状的微妙（即从"无"中去观察领悟"道"体的奥妙莫测）。总是在持有欲望趋求时，才可以观察到那母体构成的广大极致（即从"有"中去观察体会"道"用的端倪）。"无"与"有"这两者，来源相同而名称相异，都可以称之为玄妙、深远。它不是一般的玄妙、深远，而是玄妙、深远到极点，是宇宙天地万物之奥妙的门径（意指从"有名"的奥妙到达无形的奥妙，"道"是洞悉一切奥妙变化的门户）。

【英译】The Tao that can be told of is not the absolute Tao. The Names that can be given are not absolute Names. The Nameless is the origin of heaven and earth. The Named is the mother of all things. Therefore, oftentimes, one strips oneself of passion in order to see the Secret of life; Oftentimes, one regards life with passion in order to see its manifest forms. These two(the Secret and its manifestations) are in their nature the same. They are given different names when they become manifest. They may both be called the Cosmic Mystery. Reaching from the Mystery into the Deeper Mystery is the gate to the Secret of all life.

2. 【原文】天下皆知美之为美，斯恶已。皆知善之为善，斯不善已。故有无相生，难易相成，长短相较，高下相倾，音声相和，前后相随。是以圣人处无为之事，行不言之教。万物作焉而不辞，生而不有，为而不恃，功成而弗居。夫唯弗居，是以不去。

《道德经》第二章

【今译】当世人都认知到美是美的时候，丑的概念就产生了；都认知到善的时候，不善的概念也就产生了。（由上可见，一切概念、价值的判断，都是在相对的、变动的关系中产生）所以，有与无相互衍生，难和易相互成就，长和短相互形成，高和下相互包含，音和声相互应和，前和后相互跟随。因此，圣人便以"无为"（指顺其自然、摒弃人为的造作）的态度来面对世事的变化，实行"不言"（指不发号施令）的方式来施行教化；任凭万物自然生长而不加控制主导，孕育万物而不据为己有。对事物有所作为而不仗恃着自己的才能，成就自然的运作而不自居功劳。也正因他不自居功劳，所以功德、功绩才会永存，不会离开他。

【英译】When the people of the earth all know beauty as beauty, there arises the recognition of ugliness. When the people of the earth all know the good as good, there arises the recognition of evil. Therefore, Being and Non-being interdepend in growth; difficult and easy interdepend in completion; long and short interdepend in contrast; high and low interdepend in position; tones and voice interdepend in harmony; front and behind interdepend in company. Therefore the sage manages affairs without action, preaches the doctrine without words. All things take their rise, but he does not turn away from them. He gives them life, but does not take possession of them. He acts, but does not appropriate; accomplishes, but claims no credit. It is because he lays claim to no credit. It is because he lays claim to no credit, that the credit cannot be taken away from him.

3. 【原文】不尚贤，使民不争。不贵难得之货，使民不为盗。不见可欲，使民心不乱。是以圣人之治，虚其心，实其腹。弱其志，强其骨。常使民无知无欲。使夫智者不敢为也。为无为，则无不治。 　　　　　　　　　　　　　　　　　　　　《道德经》第三章

【今译】（治国者）不崇尚贤才异能，就可以使人民不生争名逐利之心；不看重稀贵难得的财货，就可以使人民不做偷盗之人；不显露足以引起贪欲的物事，就可以使人民的心志不被惑乱。因此，圣人治理天下的原则是净化人民心中的成见，满足人民的温饱需求，削弱人民的心志趋求（志，即心志，指求、争等贪婪的欲望，此乃一切智力巧诈产生之处，此乃圣人治国的阻碍，故老子主张"弱其志"），强化人民的躯体筋骨（可使人民能够努力工作，有自立自足能力）。常使人民无知无识、无欲无念，使那些巧诈机变的"智者"不敢为所欲为。只要自然依循着"无为"的原则来治政，就没有治理不好的事务了。

【英译】Exalt not the wise, so that the people shall not scheme and contend; prize not rare objects, so that the people shall not steal; shut out from sight the things of desire, so that the people's hearts shall not be disturbed. Therefore in the government of the sage, he keeps empty their hearts, makes full their bellies, discourages their ambitions, strengthens their frames so that the people may be innocent of knowledge and desires. And the cunning ones shall not presume to interfere. By action without deeds, may all live in peace.

4. 【原文】天地不仁，以万物为刍狗。圣人不仁，以百姓为刍狗。天地之间，其犹橐龠乎。虚而不屈，动而愈出。多言数穷，不如守中。 　　　　　　　　　　《道德经》第五章

【今译】天地不偏不私他的仁心（不仁，没有仁恩之心，引申为不偏不私），把万物视为刍狗一样，一视同仁，顺任万物自然生长，让它们自行荣枯。圣人不偏不私他的仁心，把百姓视作刍狗，不妄加干涉，任凭百姓自然发展，让他们自行兴衰。天地之间，实在像一具大风箱一般，它的内部虽然是虚空无物，但其作用却是无穷无尽的，愈鼓动它，风出来的也愈多，愈源源不绝。（执政者）如果政令繁杂，反会加速困窘败亡，所以倒不如以固守虚静、无为无事的原则而行。

【英译】Nature is unkind. It treats the creation like sacrificial straw-dogs. The sage is unkind. He treats the people like sacrificial straw-dogs. How the universe is like a bellows! Empty, yet it gives a supply that never fails. The more it is worked, the more it brings forth. By many words is wit exhausted. Rather, therefore, hold to the core.

5. 【原文】谷神不死，是谓玄牝。玄牝之门，是谓天地根。绵绵若存，用之不勤。

《道德经》第六章

【今译】那虚无寂静而神妙莫测的道是永恒不穷竭的，因为它具有不可思议的创生力，所以称为"玄牝"（玄牝，即不可思议的创生力。玄，幽远微妙之意。牝，指雌性的动物，此处具有母性创生作用的象征。玄牝是说"道"化生万物而不见其所以生，所以将"道"比作一种具有母性创生万物的作用的象征）。而"玄牝"的门户，就是天地的根源（道）了。道体的根源至幽至微、永续不绝，似有若无的，好像存在，但是它施展的作用却是无穷无尽。

【英译】The Spirit of the Valley never dies. It is called the Mystic Female. The Door of the Mystic Female is the root of heaven and earth. Continuously, it seems to remain. Draw upon it and it serves you with ease.

6. 【原文】天地长久。天地所以能长且久者，以其不自生，故能长生。是以圣人后其身而身先，外其身而身存。非以其无私邪？故能成其私。

《道德经》第七章

【今译】天地是长久而延续着的。天地所以能够长久，是因为它们不去强求偏私自己的生存状态（意即天地不自我执着其生。就是说如此这般也是生，如彼那般也是生，完全顺任于自然，结果天地反而不受变化所困，不去强求一种非其不可的状况去维持），所以能够持续地长久下去（长生：恒久生存）。因此，有道的圣人把自己的切身利益置后，结果反而成了众人之首（意即反而得到众人的爱戴）；把自己的身家性命置之度外，反而更能保全自己的身家性命。如此不正是因为他对自己没有偏私之心吗？这样反而更可以成就他自己。

【英译】The universe is everlasting. The reason why the universe is everlasting is that it does not live for Self. Therefore it can long endure. Therefore the sage puts himself last, and finds himself in the foremost place. Regards his body as accidental, and his body is thereby preserved. Is it not because he does not live for Self that his Self is realized?

7. 【原文】上善若水，水善利万物而不争。处众人之所恶，故几于道。居，善地。心，善渊。与，善仁。言，善信。正，善治。事，善能。动，善时。夫唯不争，故无尤。

《道德经》第八章

【今译】具有上善的人（上善：指最高境界的善德，意谓具有高尚德行的圣人）就像水一样，看似柔弱却是包容。水，善于滋养万物却不会与万物相争，总是处守于众人所厌恶的卑下之处,所以,水的特性很接近于"道"的境界。(水就像上善的人,其立身处世)居处善于择下而居,处身退让谦下;存心幽深而纯真;交游共处善于谐和相亲;言行表里如一,真诚不妄;为政善于获得卓著的成绩;处事能干而善于得到成效;行止举动善于掌握时机。正因为水总是滋养万物而不与之争的美德,所以不会引来过失怨尤。

【英译】The best of men is like water. Water benefits all things, and does not compete with them. It dwells in the lowly places that all disdain—wherein it comes near to the Tao. In his dwelling, the sage loves the lowly earth; in his heart, he loves what is profound; in his relations with others, he loves kindness; in his words, he loves sincerity; in government, he loves peace; in business affairs, he loves ability; in his actions, he loves choosing the right time. It is because he does not contend that he is without reproach.

8.【原文】持而盈之,不如其已。揣而棁之,不可长保。金玉满堂,莫之能守。富贵而骄,自遗其咎。功遂身退,天之道。 《道德经》第九章

【今译】执持累积到了盈满的状况(指过分自满自夸),不如适可而止。过分地显露锋芒,势难长保久安。即使有金玉满堂的财富,也不一定能守住。财富多又太过骄横之人,必将招致祸殃,自取其辱。功业成就之后,应该懂得收敛身退(身退:退休归隐,退身避位。凡收敛锋芒,不自恃功劳,"不有""不居"之意皆可)。这才是最合乎天道的准则。

【英译】Stretch a bow to the very full, and you will wish you had stopped in time. Temper a sword-edge to its sharpest, and the edge will not last long. When gold and jade fill your hall, you will not be able to keep them safe. To be proud with wealth and honor is to sow the seeds of one's own down-fall. Retire when your work is done, such is heaven's way.

9.【原文】三十辐共一毂,当其无,有车之用。埏埴以为器,当其无,有器之用。凿户牖以为室,当其无,有室之用。故有之以为利,无之以为用。 《道德经》第十一章

【今译】一个车轮有三十根车辐(木条),共同聚集到车轮中心的圆木上合为车毂。正因为车毂中间是虚空的,所以车子才能产生运转承载的作用。陶匠糅和黏土制作器具,正因为器具中间有虚空之处,所以器具才能产生盛物的作用。木匠开凿门窗建造房屋,正因为有了室内的空间之处,所以才能发挥了居住的作用。所以,"有"(指上述的车、器、室的实体)能带给人们便利,而"无"(指上述毂、器、室的中空之处)却能发挥它的作用。

【英译】Thirty spokes unite around the nave. From their Non-being(loss of their individuality) arises the utility of the wheel. Mold clay into a vessel. From its Non-being(the vessel's hollow) arises the utility of the vessel. Cut out doors and windows in the house(wall), from their empty space arises the utility of the house. Therefore by the existence of things we profit. And by the non-existence of things we are served.

10. 【原文】五色令人目盲，五音令人耳聋，五味令人口爽。驰骋畋猎令人心发狂。难得之货，令人行妨。是以圣人为腹不为目，故去彼取此。　　　　《道德经》第十二章

【今译】过分追求色彩缤纷的享受，会使人视觉迟钝，眼花缭乱；过分追求各种声音的享受，会使人听觉失灵，听而不闻；过分追求口腹之欲的享受，会使人味觉不敏，食不知味；过分纵情于狩猎的追逐之乐，会使人心狂荡不宁，神不守舍；过分追求稀有的金银珍宝，会使人品行不轨，伤风败德。因此，圣人的生活，只求基本的温饱，而不耽乐于声色感官的享乐。所以摒弃物欲的奢侈享受，宁取朴质宁静的精神生活。

【英译】The five colors blind the eyes of man. The five musical notes deafen the ears of man. The five flavors dull the taste of man. Horse-racing, hunting and chasing madden the minds of man. Rare, valuable goods keep their owners awake at night. Therefore the sage provides for the belly and not for the eye. Hence, he rejects the one and accepts the other.

11. 【原文】宠辱若惊，贵大患若身。　　　　《道德经》第十三章

【今译】得宠与受辱一样，都会使一个人的身心安宁受到惊扰。我们要重视这些大患，如同重视自己的身体一样。

【英译】Favor and disgrace cause one dismay. What we value and what we fear are within our Self.

12. 【原文】太上，下知有之。其次。亲而誉之。其次，畏之。其次，侮之。信不足，焉有不信焉。悠兮其贵言。功成事遂，百姓皆谓我自然。　　　　《道德经》第十七章

【今译】最高明上等的国君治理天下，使得人民不觉得有他的存在；次一等的国君，使得人民都亲近他、赞誉他；再次一等的国君，使得人民都畏惧他；最末一等的国君，使得人民都轻视他。因此，一个在上位的国君如果诚信不足，人民当然无法相信他。最高明上等的国君应该是悠闲无为，不轻易地发号施令，当人民都各安其生，天下太平成功了，万事顺遂了，人民反而都会说："我们原来自自然然就是这样的！"

【英译】Of the best rulers, the people only know that they exist, the next best they love and praise, the next they fear, and the next they revile. When they do not command the people's faith, some will lose faith in them, and then they resort to oaths! But of the best when their task is accomplished, their work done, the people all remark, "We have done it ourselves."

13. 【原文】大道废，有仁义。智慧出，有大伪。六亲不和，有孝慈。国家昏乱，有忠臣。
　　　　《道德经》第十八章

【今译】大道废弃了之后，所以才会产生提倡仁义道德的规范观念。聪明智巧（指

逐权夺利、投机取巧的诡诈）出现后，才产生狡诈和虚伪的行为来迎合。父子、兄弟、夫妇这六亲之间无法和谐相处的话，才会产生强调孝道、慈爱的观念来匡正人心。国家混乱不堪以后，才会有忠贞之臣不顾一切力挽狂澜。

【英译】On the decline of the great Tao, the doctrines of "humanity" and "justice" arose. When knowledge and cleverness appeared, great hypocrisy followed in its wake. When the six relationships no longer lived at peace, there was praise of "kind parents" and "filial sons". When a country fell into chaos and misrule, there was praise of "loyal ministers".

14.【原文】绝圣弃智，民利百倍。绝仁弃义，民复孝慈。绝巧弃利，盗贼无有。此三者以为文不足，故令有所属。见素抱朴，少私寡欲。　　　　　　《道德经》第十九章

【今译】去除聪明与抛弃智慧的虚名，人民反而可以获得百倍的益处；断绝虚假的仁，抛弃虚伪的义等束缚人们天性的道德律则，人民反而能恢复他们孝慈的本性；杜绝机巧之心与抛弃对厚利的引诱，盗贼自然就绝迹了。圣智、仁义、巧利这三者，都仅仅只是徒具虚名的文饰而已。（因为这三者）还不足以治理天下，所以，要让人民有所依归（心有所属）的话，那就外在表现纯真，内在持守着质朴，减少自己的私心，降低个人的欲望。

【英译】Banish wisdom, discard knowledge, and the people shall profit a hundredfold; banish humanity, discard justice, and the people shall recover love of their kin; banish cunning, discard utility, and the thieves and brigands shall disappear. As these three touch the externals and are inadequate, the people have need of what they can depend upon: reveal your simple Self, embrace your original nature, check your selfishness, curtail your desires.

15.【原文】人之所畏，不可不畏。　　　　　　　　　　　　《道德经》第二十章

【今译】别人所畏惧的，我们也是不可以不畏惧的，这是世事之然啊！

【英译】What men fear is indeed to be feared.

16.【原文】俗人昭昭，我独昏昏。俗人察察，我独闷闷。　　　《道德经》第二十章

【今译】世人求的是煊赫显耀，只有我是昏昏默默、不辨是非的样子。世人总是清楚精明，只有我是迷迷糊糊、不知事理的样子。

【英译】The vulgar are knowing, luminous; I alone am dull, confused. The vulgar are clever, self-assured; I alone am depressed.

17.【原文】曲则全，枉则直，洼则盈，敝则新，少则多，多则惑。是以圣人抱一为天下式。不自见故明，不自是故彰，不自伐故有功，不自矜故长。夫唯不争，故天下莫能与之争。古之所谓曲则全者，岂虚言哉！诚全而归之。　　　《道德经》第二十二章

【今译】委屈反而可以保全，弯曲反而可以伸直，低洼反而可以满盈，破旧反而可以换新，少取了反而可以有所得，多取了反而造成迷惑。因此，圣人持守着整体的

"道"，来作为天下人所学习的模范。不刻意自我表现，反而会特别显明；不刻意自以为是，反而会特别显扬；不刻意自我夸耀，反而得以功劳长存（自伐：自夸其功）；不刻意自恃自满，反而能够更加长久（自矜：自恃其能）。因为不与人争，所以天下人没有人可以和他相争。古人所说的"曲则全"（委屈反而可以保全）这样的话，哪里是虚假的空话呢？实在是应该持守着这样周全的道理，才能以之为归趋，顺应它而返于道啊！

【英译】To yield is to be preserved whole. To be bent is to become straight. To be hollow is to be filled. To be tattered is to be renewed. To be in want is to possess. To have plenty is to be confused. Therefore, the sage embraces the One, and becomes the model of the world. He does not reveal himself, and is therefore luminous. He does not justify himself, and is therefore far-famed. He does not boast of himself, and therefore, people give him credit. He does not pride himself, and is therefore the chief among men. It is because he does not contend, that no one in the world can contend against him. Is it not indeed true, as the ancients say, "to yield is to be reserved whole?" Thus he is preserved and the world does him homage.

18. 【原文】希言自然。故飘风不终朝，骤雨不终日。　　　　　《道德经》第二十三章

【今译】大道默然无言，少说话才合乎自然天成的本性，所以暴风吹刮不会持续一早晨，急雨也不会持续下一整天。

【英译】Nature says few words. Hence a squall lasts not a whole morning and a rainstorm continues not a whole day.

19. 【原文】企者不立，跨者不行，自见者不明，自是者不彰，自伐者无功，自矜者不长。

《道德经》第二十四章

【今译】踮起脚尖想站得比别人高的，反而站不稳；过度迈大步伐想走得比别人快的，反而走不远（走不动）；自求表现执求成名的人，反而不够显明；自以为是的人，反而不能清楚辨析；（因为容易遮蔽真相）自我夸耀的人，反而不见功劳（难以见功）；自骄自满的人，反而难以长久（难以成长）。

【英译】He who stands on tiptoe does not stand firm. He who strains his strides does not walk well. He who reveals himself is not luminous. He who justifies himself is not farfamed. He who boasts of himself is not given credit. He who prides himself is not chief among men.

20. 【原文】有物混成，先天地生。寂兮寥兮，独立而不改，周行而不殆，可以为天下母。吾不知其名，字之曰道，强为之名曰大。大曰逝，逝曰远，远曰反。故道大，天大，地大，王亦大。域中有四大，而王居其一焉。人法地，地法天，天法道，道法自然。

《道德经》第二十五章

【今译】有一个混然而成的东西，在天地还未创生之前即已存在。它既寂静无声息，也空虚无形体，但却独立于万物之上而恒久不变；它周而复始，运行不已地在宇宙之间；它创造天地万物，可以说是天地万物的母体本源。我不知道该如何去称呼它，就姑且叫它为"道"吧！勉强地形容它，它可说是"广大无边"。广大无边则运行不尽，运行不尽则玄远无际，玄远无际而又归返本源。这么说来，道大，天大，地大，人也大。整个宇宙之中有这四大，而人居其中的一种。人效法地的厚实涵藏，地效法天的高明宽广，天效法道的创生本源，道则是完全顺任着它自己本性中的自然精神。

【英译】Before the heaven and earth existed, there was something nebulous: silent, isolated, standing alone, changing not, eternally revolving without fail, worthy to be the Mother of all things. I do not know its name, and address it as Tao. If forced to give it a name, I shall call it "Great". Being great implies reaching out in space. Reaching out in space implies far-reaching. Far-reaching implies reversion to the original point. Therefore, Tao is great, the heaven is great, the earth is great, the king is also great. These are the Great Four in the universe, and the king is one of them. Man models himself after the earth. The earth models itself after heaven. The heaven models itself after Tao. Tao models itself after Nature.

21.【原文】重为轻根，静为躁君，是以圣人终日行，不离辎重。虽有荣观，燕处超然。奈何万乘之主，而以身轻于天下。轻则失本，躁则失君。　　《道德经》第二十六章

【今译】稳重是轻浮的根本，虚静是躁动的主宰。因此，圣人终日行走，也不离开载装行李的车辆，虽有表面上享受荣华显贵的地位，却能在日常居处时表现得从容坦荡而超脱物欲之外。为什么大国的君主，还要轻率躁动地来治理天下呢？轻率治理天下就会失去自身存在的根本，急躁妄动就会失去主控的权力。

【英译】The Solid is the root of the Light. The Quiescent is the master of the Hasty. Therefore the sage travels all day, yet never leaves his provision-cart. In the midst of honor and glory, he lives leisurely, undisturbed. How can the ruler of a great country make light of his body in the empire? In light frivolity, the Center is lost; in hasty action, self-mastery is lost.

22.【原文】知其雄，守其雌，为天下溪谷。为天下溪谷，常德不离，复归于婴儿。知其白，守其黑，为天下式。为天下式，常德不忒，复归于无极。知其荣，守其辱，为天下谷。为天下谷，常德乃足，复归于朴。朴散则为器，圣人用之，则为官长。故大制不割。

《道德经》第二十八章

【今译】虽然深知雄健刚强的道理，却宁愿持守柔弱的位置来处事，就如同甘作天下的山谷般谦下而能容，使众流归注。如同山谷般谦下而能容，就能使合于道的常德（指永恒不变之德）不会离失，而复归于婴儿状态般的纯真自然。虽然深知什么是光明豁亮的好处，却宁愿安守于晦暗的位置来行进，作为天下人共同遵守的模式。

因为是天下人共同遵守的模式，合于道的永恒之德就不会有变动偏差（忒：变更），而复归于大道的境界。虽然深知什么是荣华显耀的好处，却宁愿持守着忍辱负重的态度，如同甘作天下的山谷那样谦卑低下，能容纳天下污垢的人。甘作天下虚无宽广的山谷，就能使合于道的永恒之德充足圆满，而复归于混沌无名的纯朴状态。纯朴的道演化分散为天下万物，圣人体会运用了道的纯朴，而成为了百官之长。所以，完善的政治制度（大制：犹云大治，完善的治国之道）是顺自然而行，不会陷入支离割裂之中。

【英译】He who is aware of the Male, but keeps to the Female, becomes the ravine of the world. Being the ravine of the world, he has the original character which is not cut up, and returns again to the innocence of the babe. He who is conscious of the white(bright), but keeps to the black(dark), becomes the model for the world. Being the model for the world, he has the eternal power which never errs, and returns again to the Primordial Nothingness. He who is familiar with honor and glory, but keeps to obscurity, becomes the valley of the world. Being the valley of the world, he has an eternal power which always suffices, and returns again to the natural integrity of uncarved wood. Break up this uncarved wood, and it is shaped into vessel. In the hands of the sage, they become the officials and magistrates. Therefore the great ruler does not cut up.

23. 【原文】物壮则老，是谓不道。不道早已。　　　　　　　　　《道德经》第三十章

【今译】万事万物，一到强盛壮大到极点时，便势必开始趋于衰败，所以逞强就是不合于大道。不合于大道的事，很快就会消逝灭亡。

【英译】For things age after reaching their prime. That violence would be against the Tao. And he who is against the Tao perishes young.

24. 【原文】夫佳兵者，不祥之器，物或恶之，故有道者不处……吉事尚左，凶事尚右，偏将军居左，上将军居右，言以丧礼处之。　　　　　《道德经》第三十一章

【今译】锐利的兵器，是个不吉祥的器物。人们多半都厌恶它，因此，有道之士是不会使用、接纳它的……自古以来，吉庆之事以左方为大位，凶丧之事则以右方为大位。同样道理，用兵时偏将军（指副统帅）居于左方，上将军（主帅）居于右方。这说明把用兵作战一事等同于丧事来看待。

【英译】Of all things, weapons are instruments of evil, hated by men. Therefore the religious man possessed of Tao avoids them…The things of good omen favor the left. The things of ill omen favor the right. The lieutenant-general stands on the left. The general stands on the right. That is to say, it is celebrated as a Funeral Rite.

25. 【原文】天地相合，以降甘露。民莫之令而自均。始制有名，名亦既有，夫亦将知止。

知止可以不殆。譬道之在天下，犹川谷之于江海。　　　　　　《道德经》第三十二章

【今译】天地的阴阳之气相合，自然就会降下甘露。人民不须指使它，它就会到达自然均匀的状态。大道创造了万物，有物必有形，万物开始有了名称去建制这个世界，名称既已产生，纷争也会跟着产生，所以要能够知道适可而止。能够知道适可而止，这样才能免除危险。大道之无心流布于天下万物，而万物却仍自归于大道，就好像江海是百川的归宿一样，百川终将自动流归江海。

【英译】The heaven and earth join, and the sweet rain falls, beyond the command of men, yet evenly upon all. Then human civilization arises and there are names. Since there are names, one should know where to stop. He who knows where to stop may be exempt from danger. Tao in the world may be compared to rivers that run into the sea.

26. 【原文】知人者智，自知者明。胜人者有力，自胜者强。知足者富，强行者有志。不失其所者久，死而不亡者寿。　　　　　　《道德经》第三十三章

【今译】能够了解别人的善恶长短的，可称之聪慧；能够认识自己良知本性的，可称之聪明（指清明而有悟性）。能够胜过别人的，可谓之有力；能够胜过自己的，可谓之强者。能够知足而淡泊名利的，就算是富有；能够坚持力行大道而亘久不息的，就算是有志（确立了志向）。常处于大道，不离失它所维系、归依的所在根基，才能长久；身躯虽死却能与道同存，就谓之长寿。

【英译】He who knows others is learned. He who knows himself is wise. He who conquers others has power of muscles. He who conquers himself is strong. He who is contented is rich. He who is determined has strength of will. He who does not lose his center endures. He who dies yet his power remains has long life.

27. 【原文】将欲歙之，必固张之。将欲弱之，必固强之。将欲废之，必固兴之。将欲夺之，必固与之。是谓微明，柔弱胜刚强。鱼不可脱于渊，国之利器不可以示人。

《道德经》第三十六章

【今译】对于任何事物，想要收敛它，必须先去扩张它。想要削弱它，必须先去增强它。想要废弃它，必须先去兴举它。想要夺取它，必须先去给予它。这个道理看似隐微不引人注意，其实很明显。这正是柔弱胜过刚强的道理所在：鱼不能离开深渊之水而生存，以免干涸而死；有利于国家的事物不可轻易展示于人，以免为人所夺，国灭身亡。

【英译】He who is to be made to dwindle in power must first be caused to expand. He who is to be weakened must first be made strong. He who is to be laid low must first be exalted to power. He who is to be taken away from must first be given. This is the Subtle Light. Gentleness overcomes strength: fish should be left in the deep pool, and sharp weapons of the state should be left where none can see them.

28. 【原文】道常无为而无不为。 《道德经》第三十七章

    【今译】自然的大道通常什么也不作为，却又没有东西不是出于它的作为。

    【英译】The Tao never does, yet through it everything is done.

29. 【原文】上德不德，是以有德。下德不失德，是以无德。上德无为，而无以为。下德为之，而有以为。上仁为之，而无以为。上义为之，而有以为。上礼为之，而莫之应，则攘臂而扔之。故失道而后德，失德而后仁，失仁而后义，失义而后礼。夫礼者，忠信之薄，而乱之首。 《道德经》第三十八章

    【今译】具有上德的人，一切依道而行，并不刻意彰显德名，因此反而有德；具有下德的人，念念不忘张扬德名以示不失德，因此反而无法拥有高尚的品德。具有上德的人，顺应自然不刻意作为，因此也无心作为；具有下德的人，虽依顺自然无为，实际上却是有心作为。具有上仁之心的人，诚身而行，虽有作为却是不恃德名，所以是无所求的作为。具有上义之心的人，一切作为都是为了责任正义，凡事计较是非曲直，所以是有所求的作为。具有上礼的人，制定各种礼仪节度的作为并身体力行，如果得不到相对的响应，他便会举起手臂来，引领人们来遵守礼节，强迫别人顺从。如此看来，失去了道才会有德，失去了德才会有仁，失去了仁才会有义，失去了义才要讲求，而礼仪规范这些东西，是人性由忠诚、信实为其主要内涵而转趋淡薄的表现，这正是社会由安定趋于混乱的开始。

    【英译】The man of superior character is not conscious of his character, hence he has character. The man of inferior character is intent on not losing character, hence he is devoid of character. The man of superior character never acts, nor ever does so with an ulterior motive. The man of inferior character acts, and does so with an ulterior motive. The man of superior kindness acts, but does so without an ulterior motive. The man of superior justice acts, and does so with an ulterior motive. But when the man of superior Li acts and finds no response, he rolls up his sleeves to force it on others. Therefore, after Tao is lost, then arises the doctrine of humanity; after humanity is lost, then arises the doctrine of kindness, after kindness is lost, then arises the doctrine of justice, after justice is lost, then arises the doctrine of Li. Now Li is the thinning out of loyalty and honesty of heart, and the beginning of chaos.

30. 【原文】昔之得一者，天得一以清，地得一以宁，神得一以灵，谷得一以盈，万物得一以生，侯王得一以为天下贞。 《道德经》第三十九章

    【今译】自古以来，凡是能拥有大道而浑融一体的：天由于得到一因而才清明，地由于得到一因而才宁静，神由于得到一因而才显现灵通，谷由于得到一因而才充盈，

万物由于得到一因而才生长，侯王由于得到一因而才成为天下的君主。

【英译】There were those in ancient times possessed of the One: through possession of the One, the heaven was clarified; through possession of the One, the earth was stabilized; through possession of the One, the gods were spiritualized; through possession of the One, the valleys were made full; through possession of the One, all things lived and grew; through possession of the One, the princes and dukes became the ennobled of the people.

31. 【原文】天下之物生于有，有生于无。 《道德经》第四十章

【今译】天下万物各种物类的存在，都是从"有"产生的，而"有"是从"无"产生的。

【英译】The things of this world come from Being, and Being comes from Non-being.

32. 【原文】上士闻道，勤而行之。中士闻道，若存若忘。下士闻道，大笑之。不笑不足以为道。故建言有之：明道若昧，进道若退，夷道若纇。上德若谷，大白若辱，广德若不足，建德若偷，质真若渝。大方无隅，大器晚成，大音希声，大象无形，道隐无名，夫唯道善贷且成。 《道德经》第四十一章

【今译】上等资质的人听说了"道"，即会努力地去实践；中等资质的人听说了"道"，则持着半信半疑的态度；下等资质的人听说了"道"，便会大笑起来——如果他们没笑，那就不足以被称为"道"了。所以古时候立言的人说过：真正了解"道"的人，看起来是愚昧不明的；在真正的"道"上前进的人，看起来就好像在退后；在平坦的"道"上前进的人，看起来就好像是在崎岖不平的路上行走。上等的德是谦冲的，如同山谷一般；心灵如同最纯洁的白色却看来像是藏污纳垢；最广博的德却好像有所不足；最坚实的德却好像不甚牢固；最质朴的德却好像会随着外物而改变；最方正的东西其实没有棱角；最大的器皿其实是最后才制成的；最大的声音其实听来没有声响；最大的形象其实是看不见形状的；而真正的道就是退隐于后，而没有名称可言。也只有道，善于施与万物并成就一切。

【英译】When the highest type of men hear the Tao(truth), they try hard to live in accordance with it; when the mediocre type hear the Tao, they seem to be aware and yet unaware of it; when the lowest type hear the Tao, they break into loud laughter—if it were not laughed at, it would not be Tao. Therefore, there is the established saying—he who understands Tao seems dull of comprehension; who is advanced in Tao seems to slip backwards; who moves on the even Tao path seems to go up and down. Superior character appears like a hollow(valley). Sheer white appears like tarnished. Great character appears like insufficient. Solid character appears like infirm. Pure worth appears like contaminated. Great space has no corners. Great talent takes long to mature. Great music is faintly heard. Great form has no contour. And Tao is hidden without a name. It is this Tao that is adept at lending its power and bringing fulfillment.

33. 【原文】道生一，一生二，二生三，三生万物。万物负阴而抱阳，冲气以为和。人之所恶，唯孤、寡不穀，而侯王以为称，故物或损之而益，或益之而损。人之所教，我亦教之。强梁者不得其死，吾将以为教父。　　　　　　　　　　《道德经》第四十二章

【今译】由道而生成了一（"一"者，即为气，指宇宙所混合而成的一个调和而均匀的整体），再由一生成了二（"二"者，即宇宙中的阴阳二气），二再生成三（"三"者，指阴阳二气交流所产生的"和"。此为老子学说中最著名的万物生成论，描述道的生成是由简至繁的、一、二、三即是在表示愈生愈多，以至于万物。再者，道本身是无以名状的，而生成的一、二、三以至于万物则是有名有状，故亦是在表述有无相生之理），而三再产生了万物（天、地、和三者使得万物得以生成）。万物的变化大多是背着阴而面对阳的，再经由阴阳二气的互相激荡（"冲"气：此作"激荡"解。此之阴阳二气，指的是两种不同性质的物质，亦是万物赖以生存的根本；阴气是指沉重浑浊的纯物质，阳气则指的是赋予万物生命的精华）来达到彼此的和谐。人们所厌恶的，不外乎是那些孤家寡人及不善之人，但那些王公贵族却是如此称呼自己，这就是因为宇宙万物的变化，有的时候是在受损中得到增益，但有的时候则因为想使它增益却反而导致受损。这是别人教导我的，此时我也以此来教导别人：强悍的人（"强梁者"：即"强暴者"，指强行霸道的人。此句为周朝金人的铭文，为古人用来教诲人的句子，故老子于文中有如此说法）是没有办法得到善终的我将把这句话当作一切施教的精神准则。

【英译】Out of Tao, one is born; out of one, two; out of two, three; out of three, the created universe. The created universe carries the Yin at its back and the Yang in front. Through the union of the pervading principles, it reaches harmony. To be "orphaned" "lonely" and "unworthy" is what men hate most. Yet the princes and dukes call themselves by such names. For sometimes things are benefited by being taken away from, and suffer by being added to. Others have taught this maxim, which I shall teach also, "The violent man shall die a violent death." This I shall regard as my spiritual teacher.

34. 【原文】天下之至柔，驰骋天下之至坚。无有入无间，吾是以知无为之有益。不言之教，无为之益，天下希及之。　　　　　　　　　　　　　　　　《道德经》第四十三章

【今译】全天下最柔弱的东西可以畅行无阻于天底下最坚硬的东西。也就是以无形的力量穿透了坚实而没有间隙的东西。我因此知道了无所作为的好处。然而不用言语的教导和无所作为的好处，天底下却是很少人可以做得到。

【英译】The softest substance of the world goes through the hardest. That which is without form penetrates that which has no crevice. Through this I know the benefit of taking no action. The teaching without words and the benefit of taking no action are without compare in the universe.

35. 【原文】名与身孰亲？身与货孰多？得与亡孰病？是故甚爱必大费，多藏必厚亡。知足不辱，知止不殆，可以长久。　　　　　　　　　　《道德经》第四十四章

【今译】名誉和身体，哪一个和我们比较亲近？身体与财货，哪一个对我们来说比较重要？获得与失去，哪一个对我们来说比较有害？所以说过分的爱惜，一定会大费心思；积藏过多的财货，而后必定会导致惨痛的损失。知道满足，就不会招致羞辱；知道停止，就不会遇上危险，这样才可以让生命平安长久。

【英译】Fame or one's own Self, which does one love more? One's own Self or material goods, which has more worth? Loss of Self or possession of goods, which is the greater evil? Therefore, he who loves most spends most and he who hoards much loses much. The contented man meets no disgrace, who knows when to stop runs into no danger—he can long endure.

36. 【原文】大成若缺，其用不弊。大盈若冲，其用不穷。大直若屈，大巧若拙，大辩若讷。躁胜寒，静胜热。静为天下正。　　　　　　　　《道德经》第四十五章

【今译】最大的圆满，往往看起来就好像有所空陷，但它的作用是不会有问题的；最大的满盈，往往看起来就好像很空虚似的，但它的作用是不会穷尽的；最直的直线，却往往看起来是弯曲的；最灵巧的技术，却往往看起来是笨拙的；最高明的辩才，却往往看起来是木讷的。躁动可以克服寒冷，清静可以克服炎热。因此，清静无为才是天下的正途。

【英译】The highest perfection is like imperfection, and its use is never impaired. The greatest abundance seems meager, and its use will never fail. What is most straight appears devious. The greatest skill appears like clumsiness. The greatest eloquence seems like stuttering. Movement overcomes cold, but keeping still overcomes heat. Who is calm and quiet becomes the guide for the universe.

37. 【原文】天下有道，却走马以粪。天下无道，戎马生于郊。祸莫大于不知足，咎莫大于欲得。故知足之足，常足矣。　　　　　　　　　　《道德经》第四十六章

【今译】当天下实行"道治"的时候，就可遣退战马不用，转而送往农村运送粪肥到田里耕种。当天下没有实行"道治"的时候，则战马就会生于战场的郊野。一切的祸害没有比不知足更为严重的了，一切的过错也不会大过什么都想要得到。所以要是能在内心拥有知足的这种满足，就能够永远满足了。

【英译】When the world lives in accord with Tao, racing horses are turned back to haul refuse carts. When the world lives not in accord with Tao, cavalry abounds in the countryside. There is no greater curse than the lack of contentment, no greater sin than the desire for possession.

Therefore he who is contented with contentment shall be always content.

38.【原文】不出户，知天下。不窥牖，见天道。其出弥远，其知弥少。是以圣人不行而知，不见而名，不为而成。　　　　　　　　　　　　　　　　　　　　《道德经》第四十七章

【今译】不出门，就可以知道天下之事。不望向窗外，就可以看见天下的自然规律（此指掌握自然界运行法则的人，即可透析事物的真实状况）。一个人走得越远，所认知的事物真相就越少（此指不了解自然界运行法则的人，心愈是躁动，愈是难以明了外界事物）。所以圣贤之人不用出门远行就可以知道事物的真相，不用亲眼去看就可以明白事物的变化，不用有所作为就可以成就大业。

【英译】Without stepping outside one's doors, one can know what is happening in the world; without looking out of one's window, one can see the Tao of heaven. The farther one pursues knowledge, the less one knows. Therefore, the sage knows without running about, understands without seeing, accomplishes without doing.

39.【原文】为学日益，为道日损。损之又损，以至于无为，无为而无不为。取天下常以无事。及其有事，不足以取天下。　　　　　　　　　　　　　　《道德经》第四十八章

【今译】探求学问知识，每天都会学得更多一些；但探求"道"，则每天的作为都会减少一些。而且减少之后还要再减少，最后达到无所作为（顺应自然）的境界。然而无所作为却又其实什么事情都可以做。治理天下就应常常无所作为。一旦真的需要有所作为，那就不配治理天下了。

【英译】The student of knowledge aims at learning day by day; the student of Tao aims at losing day by day. By continual losing, one reaches doing nothing. By doing nothing, everything is done. He who conquers the world often does so by doing nothing. When one is compelled to do something, the world is already beyond his conquering.

40.【原文】圣人无常心，以百姓心为心。善者，吾善之，不善者，吾亦善之，德善。信者，吾信之，不信者，吾亦信之，德信。圣人在天下，歙歙，为天下浑其心，圣人皆孩之。

《道德经》第四十九章

【今译】圣贤之人治国处事时不会带有主观成见，且会时时挂念着人民的想法。善良的人我会善待他，而不善良的人我也会善待他。如此一来，人人就都会视善良为美德。有诚信的人我相信他，没有诚信的人我也相信他。如此一来，人人也都会以诚信为美德了。圣贤之人立身于天下，是非常谨慎收敛的。使天下人心都能多归于浑厚纯朴，圣人就把百姓都视作孩童一般对待。

【英译】The sage has no decided opinions and feelings, but regards the people's opinions and feelings as his own. The good ones I declare good; the bad ones I also declare good. That is the goodness of Virtue. The honest ones I believe; the liars I also believe. That is the faith of Virtue. The sage dwells in the world peacefully, harmoniously. The people of the world are brought into a community of heart, and the sage regards them all as his own children.

41.【原文】出生入死，生之徒十有三，死之徒十有三。人之生，动之死地亦十有三。夫何故？以其生生之厚。 《道德经》第五十章

【今译】人是从出生开始，再慢慢走向死亡的。其中长寿的人占了十分之三，而短命的人也占了十分之三。人们希望能够长寿，却因过度的保养、恣意妄为而使自己提早步入死亡的，也是占了十分之三。这是什么原因呢？就是因为他们太过于厚待自己了。

【英译】Out of life, death enters. The companions(organs) of life are three-tenths. The companions(organs) of death are also three-tenths. What send man to death in this life is also three-tenths. How is it so? Because of the intense activity of multiplying life.

42.【原文】道生之，德畜之，物形之，势成之。是以万物莫不尊道而贵德。道之尊，德之贵，夫莫之命而常自然。故道生之，德畜之，长之、育之，亭之、毒之，养之、覆之。生而不有，为而不恃，长而不宰，是谓玄德。 《道德经》第五十一章

【今译】大道生出万物，再由德来滋养，物质赋予了万物形体，再借由环境来使万物长成。所以万物无不是尊崇道而珍视德的。对大道尊崇，对德珍视，就是因为他们从未发号任何的命令，向来是顺应自然的。所以说大道产生万物，由德来畜养，让万物成长、发育，使万物成熟，对万物加以抚育、爱护。创造了万物却不占为己有，化育万物却不自恃才能，生长万物却不会主宰万物——这就叫作玄德（玄德：一指潜藏而不着于外的德性，亦指自然无为的德性）。

【英译】Tao gives them birth. Teh(Character) fosters them. The material world gives them form. The circumstances of the moment complete them. Therefore, all things of the universe worship Tao and exalt Teh. Tao is worshipped and Teh is exalted without anyone's order but is so of their own accord. Therefore Tao gives them birth and Teh fosters them, makes them grow, develops them, gives them a harbor, a place to dwell in peace, feeds them and shelters them. It gives them birth and does not own them, acts and does not appropriate them, is superior, and does not control them—this is the Mystic Virtue.

43.【原文】修之于身，其德乃真。修之于家，其德乃余。修之于乡，其德乃长。修之于国，其德乃丰。修之于天下，其德乃普。故以身观身，以家观家，以乡观乡，以国观国，以天下观天下。吾何以知天下之然哉？以此。 《道德经》第五十四章

【今译】一个人能修持正道于己身，他的德行才会是真实的；能推广正道于整个家中，他的德行才是真的绰绰有余；能推广正道于整个乡里，他的德行才能够有所增长；

能推广正道于整个国家，他的德行才能够更加丰厚；能推广正道于全天下，他的德行才能够加以普及。所以，以一个人的言行表现，来观察那人的修养；以一个家庭的道德规范，来观察这个家庭的修德；以一个乡里的风俗习惯，来观察这个乡里的修德；以一个国家的兴盛衰败，去观察这个国家的修德；以全天下的风潮，去观察这个天下的修德。我如何知道全天下是不是修德了呢？就是用这样一步步观察的方式来明白的。

【英译】Cultivated in the individual, character will become genuine; cultivated in the family, character will become abundant; cultivated in the village, character will multiply; cultivated in the state, character will prosper; cultivated in the world, character will become universal. Therefore, according to the character of the individual, judge the individual; according to the character of the family, judge the family; according to the character of the village, judge the village; according to the character of the state, judge the state; according to the character of the world, judge the world. How do I know the world is so? By this.

44.**【原文】**知者不言，言者不知。塞其兑，闭其门，挫其锐，解其分，和其光，同其尘，是谓玄同。故不可得而亲，不可得而疏，不可得而利，不可得而害，不可得而贵，不可得而贱，故为天下贵。

《道德经》第五十六章

【今译】真正理解大道的人，是不会到处去说的；会到处去说的，就不是真正了解大道的人。堵塞住感官的欲望，关上欲望进出的门户，收敛本身的锐气，解开思绪的纷杂，隐藏住外露的光芒，和尘垢相混合——这就是所谓的"玄同"。因此，人们无法与他亲近，也无法和他疏远；不会让他获得好处，也不会使他受害；不会让他变得高贵，也不会使他卑贱，所以他才是天下最尊贵的人。

【英译】He who knows does not speak. He who speaks does not know. Fill up its apertures, close its doors, dull its edges, untie its tangles, soften its light, submerge its turmoil—this is the Mystic Unity. Then love and hatred cannot touch him. Profit and loss cannot reach him. Honor and disgrace cannot affect him. Therefore, he is always the honored one of the world.

45.**【原文】**以正治国，以奇用兵，以无事取天下。吾何以知其然哉？以此：天下多忌讳，而民弥贫，民多利器，国家滋昏；人多伎巧，奇物滋起；法令滋彰，盗贼多有。故圣人云，我无为而民自化，我好静而民自正，我无事而民自富，我无欲，而民自朴。

《道德经》第五十七章

【今译】以正大光明的方式来治理国家，以奇诡诈谋来领兵作战，再以无所事事来治理天下。我从何知道这个道理呢？我是依照这几个事实来看。天下禁忌愈多，人民就会愈贫苦。人民拥有的刀剑武器愈多，就显得这个国家愈加昏庸无能。人的技术巧智愈多，怪事就会愈多。国家的法令愈严苛，盗贼也就会变得愈多。所以圣人

43

说道：" 我因为无所作为而使得人民自然发展。我喜欢清静，则人民自然而然就会端正品行。我无所事事，而人民自然而然就会富足。我无欲无求，而人民自然而然就会淳朴敦厚。"

【英译】Rule a kingdom by the normal. Fight a battle by abnormal tactics of surprise. Win the world by doing nothing. How do I know it is so? Through this: the more prohibitions there are, the poorer the people become; the more sharp weapons there are, the greater the chaos in the state; the more skills of technique, the more cunning things are produced; the greater the number of statutes, the greater the number of thieves and brigands. Therefore, the sage says, "I do nothing and the people are reformed of themselves. I love quietude and the people are righteous of themselves. I deal in no business and the people grow rich by themselves. I have no desires and the people are simple and honest by themselves."

46.【原文】祸兮福之所倚，福兮祸之所伏。孰知其极？其无正？正复为奇，善复为妖。人之迷，其日固久。是以圣人方而不割，廉而不刿，直而不肆，光而不耀。

《道德经》第五十八章

【今译】灾祸，常倚伴在福祉的旁边；福祉，则常是灾祸所潜伏之处。谁能知道这究竟是怎么回事呢？这就是因为祸福没有一定的常理。正面的事物有时会变成反面，善良有时会变成邪恶。人们的迷惑，也已经有很长一段时间了。因此圣人表现出来的方正，不会去割伤别人，虽然为人清廉，却不会去伤害别人；虽然行为直率，却不会盛气凌人；虽是光芒四射，却不会耀眼刺人。

【英译】Disaster is the avenue of fortune, and fortune is the concealment for disaster. Who would be able to know its ultimate results? As it is, there would never be the normal, but the normal would immediately revert to the deceitful, and the good revert to the sinister. Thus long has mankind gone astray! Therefore, the sage who is square has firm principles, but not cutting sharp-cornered, has integrity but does not hurt others, is straight, but not high-handed, bright, but not dazzling.

47.【原文】治大国若烹小鲜。 《道德经》第六十章

【今译】治理一个大的国家，要像是在烹调小鱼一般。

【英译】Rule a big country as you would fry small fish.

48.【原文】大国者下流，天下之交，天下之牝，牝常以静胜牡，以静为下。故大国以下小国，则取小国。小国以下大国，则取大国。故或下以取，或下而取。大国不过欲兼畜人，小国不过欲入事人，夫两者各得其所欲，大者宜为下。

《道德经》第六十一章

【今译】大的国家应该要像是江海一般位于河流的下游，为天下河流的交汇点。就

要如同天下间的雌性动物，雌性动物常以安静来胜过雄性动物，就是因为安静，所以能够处于下位。所以大国若是可以用谦卑来对待小国，就可以取得小国的信赖；相对的，如果小国能够用谦卑来对待大国，也可以取得大国的信任。所以有的是以谦下来取信，有的则是以谦下而取信。大国只不过是想要小国成为附庸国，小国也只不过是想要事奉大国而取得大国的保护。大国和小国都满足了各自的愿望，而大国尤其应当要谦下。

【英译】A big country should be like the delta low-regions, being the concourse of the world, and the Female of the world. The Female overcomes the Male by quietude, and achieves the lowly position by quietude. Therefore, if a big country places itself below a small country, it absorbs the small country; and if a small country places itself below a big country, it absorbs the big country. Therefore, some place themselves low to absorb others, some are naturally low and absorb others. What a big country wants is nothing but to shelter others, and what a small country wants is nothing but to be able to come in and be sheltered. Thus considering that both may have what they want, a big country ought to place itself low.

49.【原文】为无为，事无事，味无味。大小多少，报怨以德。图难于其易，为大于其细。天下难事，必作于易。天下大事，必作于细。是以圣人终不为大，故能成其大。夫轻诺必寡信，多易必多难。是以圣人犹难之，故终无难矣。　　《道德经》第六十三章

【今译】把无为当成作为，把没事当作有事，把恬淡无味当作有滋味。不去计较大小多少，以仁德来回报怨恨。解决困难要从简单的开始，做大事则要从小处开始着手。天下间的难事，一定是始于简单容易的地方；天下间的大事，也一定是从微小之处开始。所以圣人始终不做大事，因此能成就他的大业；轻易地许下承诺的人，一定会缺乏诚信。将事情看得太容易，则必定会遇到更多的困难。圣人因为将任何事都看得很困难，所以最后就会显得毫无困难了。

【英译】Accomplish do-nothing. Attend to no-affairs. Taste the flavorless. Whether it is big or small, many or few, requite hatred with virtue. Deal with the difficult while yet it is easy; deal with the big while yet it is small. The difficult problems of the world must be dealt with while they are yet easy; the great problem of the world must be dealt with while they are yet small. Therefore the sage by never dealing with great problems accomplishes greatness. He who lightly makes a promise will find it often hard to keep his faith; he who makes light of many things will encounter many difficulties. Hence even the sage regards things as difficult, and for that reason never meets with difficulties.

50.【原文】其安易持，其未兆易谋。其脆易泮，其微易散。为之于未有，治之于未乱。合抱之木，生于毫末。九层之台，起于累土。千里之行，始于足下。为者败之，执

者失之。是以圣人无为，故无败。无执，故无失。民之从事，常于几成而败之。慎终如始，则无败事。是以圣人欲不欲，不贵难得之货。学不学，复众人之所过。以辅万物之自然，而不敢为。 　　　　　　《道德经》第六十四章

【今译】情势安定时比较容易掌握，事情在还没有征兆之前比较容易应付，事物在脆弱时就容易破碎，东西在还微小的时候就容易散乱。当事情尚未发生之时就先处理好，在灾乱还没发生之时就先采取应有的措施。双手合抱的大树，也是生于细小的嫩芽；九层楼高的高台，也是一筐筐的土累积而筑起的；千里的远行，也是一步一步走出来的。有作为的，终将会失败；执着的人，总是容易失去。所以圣人无所作为，因此而不会失败；不去执着，所以不容易失去。人们做的事，常常在几乎要成功时最后反而失败。若是在事情结束时，都能够一如开始时的谨慎小心，就不会有失败的机会。所以圣人希望人们可以抛弃欲望，不过于重视难得一见的财货；学习不被看重的学问，以弥补人们所犯的过错，来助成万物的自然成长，而不敢强为。

【英译】That which lies still is easy to hold. That which is not yet manifest is easy to forestall. That which is brittle like ice easily melts. That which is minute easily scatters. Deal with a thing before it is there. Check disorder before it is rife. A tree with a full span's girth begins from a tiny sprout. A nine-storied terrace begins with a clod of earth. A journey of a thousand li begins at one's feet. He who acts, spoils; he who grasps, lets slip. Because the sage does not act, he does not spoil; because he does not grasp, he does not let slip. The affairs of men are often spoiled within an ace of completion. By being careful at the end as at the beginning, failure is averted. Therefore the sage desires to have no desire, and values not objects difficult to obtain, learns what is unlearned, and restores what the multitude have lost, that he may assist in the course of nature, and not presume to interfere.

51.【原文】古之善为道者，非以明民，将以愚之。民之难治，以其智多。故以智治国，国之贼。不以智治国，国之福。 　　　　　　《道德经》第六十五章

【今译】古时候善于推行"道"的人，不是用道来启发人民的智慧，而是用道来让人民愚昧。人民之所以难以治理，就是因为拥有太多的知识，所以用知识来治理国家的人，是国家的灾祸；不用知识来治理国家的人，才是国家的福气。

【英译】The ancients who knew how to follow the Tao aimed not to enlighten the people, but to keep them ignorant. The reason why it is difficult for the people to live in peace is because of too much knowledge. Those who seek to rule a country by knowledge are the nation's curse. Those who seek not to rule a country by knowledge are the nation's blessing.

52. 【原文】江海所以能为百谷王者，以其善下之。故能为百谷王。是以欲上民必以言下之，欲先民必以身后之。是以圣人处上而民不重，处前而民不害。是以天下乐推而不厌。以其不争，故天下莫能与之争。

《道德经》第六十六章

【今译】江海之所以可以成为天下江河的汇归，就是因为它善于屈居低下的位置，所以才能让百川归往。因此想要身居万民之上，就必须要言语谦下；想要身在万民之前，就必须能退在人民之后。因此圣人虽身处在万人之上，人民也不会感到沉重；虽身处万人之前，人民也不会觉得有害。所以天下人乐于拥戴他而不会厌恶他。就是因为他不会与人相争，所以天下就无人能与他相争了。

【英译】How did the great rivers and seas become the lords of the ravines? By being good at keeping low. That was how they became the lords of the ravines. Therefore, in order to be the chief among the people, one must speak like their inferiors. In order to be foremost among the people, one must walk behind them. Thus it is that the sage stays above, and the people do not feel his weight; walk in front, and the people do not wish him harm. Then the people of the world are glad to uphold him forever. Because he does not contend, no one in the world can contend against him.

53. 【原文】我有三宝，持而保之。一曰慈，二曰俭，三曰不敢为天先。

《道德经》第六十七章

【今译】我有三个宝物，一直掌握且保持着：一是仁慈，二是俭约，三是不敢身居于天下人之前。

【英译】I have three treasures to guard and keep them safe: the first is love; the second is, never too much; the third is, never be the first in the world.

54. 【原文】祸莫大于轻敌，轻敌几丧吾宝。故抗兵相加，哀者胜矣。

《道德经》第六十九章

【今译】在战场上，最大的灾祸就是看轻敌人，看轻敌人则会丧失作战的法宝。所以两军对战之际，有哀悯之心的一方就会获得胜利。

【英译】There is no greater catastrophe than to underestimate the enemy. To underestimate the enemy might entail the loss of my treasures. Therefore when two equally matched armies meet, it is the man of sorrow who wins.

55. 【原文】知不知，上。不知知，病。夫唯病病，是以不病。圣人不病。以其病病，是以不病。

《道德经》第七十一章

【今译】知道却不说自己知道的人，是最上等的人；明明不知道，却说自己已经知道的人，就是有毛病的人。正因为把这种毛病视作病态，所以才不会有这样的毛病。圣人没有如此的毛病。就是因为他把这种毛病视作是病态，所以才会没有这样的毛病。

【英译】One who knows that he does not know is the highest. One who pretends to know what he does not know is sick-minded. And one who recognizes sick-mindedness as sick-mindedness is not sick-minded. The sage is not sick-minded. Because he recognizes sick-mindedness as sick mindedness, therefore he is not sick-minded.

56. 【原文】民不畏威，则大威至。无狎其所居，无厌其所生。夫唯不厌，是以不厌。是以圣人自知，不自见。自爱，不自贵。故去彼取此。　　《道德经》第七十二章

【今译】当人民不畏惧威势的时候，就是更大的威胁到来的时候。不去束缚人民的日常起居，不去压榨人民的生存物资。正因为不去压迫人民，所以才不会被人民所厌恶。因此圣人自己了解自己，却不去显扬自己；爱惜自己，却不会自以为尊贵。所以才会去除自见、自贵的做法，采取不自见、不自贵的作风。

【英译】When people have no fear of force, then as is the common practice great force descends upon them. Despise not their dwellings. Dislike not their progeny. Because you do not dislike them, you yourself will not be disliked. Therefore the sage knows himself, but does not show himself; loves himself, but does not exalt himself. Therefore he rejects one force and accepts the other gentility.

57. 【原文】天网恢恢，疏而不失。　　《道德经》第七十三章

【今译】道就如同一面广大无边的网，虽然这面网是疏松的却不会有丝毫的遗漏。

【英译】The heaven's net is broad and wide. With big meshes, yet letting nothing slip through.

58. 【原文】人之生也柔弱，其死也坚强。万物草木之生也柔脆，其死也枯槁。故坚强者死之徒，柔弱者生之徒。是以兵强则不胜。木强则兵。强大处下，柔弱处上。

《道德经》第七十六章

【今译】人刚出生的时候身体是柔软的，而死后才会变得僵硬。万物草木在活着的时候枝叶是柔脆的，死去了才会枯槁坚硬。所以只要是坚强的，往往是死亡的一类；而柔弱的，才往往是属于生存的一类。因此兵力强大就不会得胜。树木壮大了就容易被砍伐。可见强大的就会居于劣势，柔弱的就会处于优势。

【英译】When man is born, he is tender and weak. At death, he is hard and stiff. When the things and plants are alive, they are soft and supple. When they are dead, they are brittle and dry. Therefore hardness and stiffness are the companions of death, and softness and gentleness are the companions of life. Therefore when an army is headstrong, it will lose in battle. When a tree is hard, it will be cut down. The big and strong belong underneath. The gentle and weak belong at the top.

59. 【原文】天下莫柔弱于水，而攻坚强者莫之能胜，以其无以易之。弱之胜强，柔之胜刚，天下莫不知，莫能行。　　《道德经》第七十八章

【今译】天下间没有什么是比水更加柔弱的了，但是要攻破坚强事物，却也没有什么可以胜过水了，因为水的本质是没有东西可以改变的。弱之所以胜强，柔之所以克刚，全天下没有人不知道，却没有人能够做得到。

【英译】There is nothing weaker than water, but none is superior to it in overcoming the hard, for which there is no substitute. Weakness overcomes strength, and gentleness overcomes rigidity. No one does not know it but no one can put it into practice.

60.【原文】小国寡民，使有什伯之器而不用，使民重死而不远徙。虽有舟舆，无所乘之。虽有甲兵，无所陈之。使人复结绳而用之。甘其食，美其服，安其居，乐其俗。邻国相望，鸡犬之声相闻，民至老死不相往来。　　　　　　　　　　《道德经》第八十章

【今译】国土小，人民少，即使有供十人、百人所用的器物也无处可以使用，让人民爱惜自己的生命而不愿远走他乡；虽然有船只、车辆，也没有必要乘坐。即使有盔甲、兵器，也没有必要去使用；使人民重新使用结绳记事的方法；有甘甜的美食，有华美的服饰，可以住得很安逸，乐于当下的风俗环境；和邻近的国家彼此相望（距离很近），两国鸡鸣狗吠的声音彼此都可以听得到，两国的人民一直到老去过世都不相往来。

【英译】Let there be a small country with a small population, where the supply of goods are tenfold or hundredfold, more than they can use. Let the people value their lives and not migrate far. Be there boats and carriages, there is no one to ride them. Be there armor and weapons, there is no occasion to display them. Let the people again tie ropes for reckoning. Let them enjoy their food, beautify their clothing, be satisfied with their homes, delight in their customs. The neighboring settlements overlook one another. So that they can hear the barking of dogs and crowing of cocks of their neighbors, and the people till the end of their days shall never have been outside their country.

61.【原文】信言不美，美言不信。善者不辩，辩者不善。知者不博，博者不知……天之道，利而不害。圣人之道，为而不争。　　　　　　　　　　《道德经》第八十一章

【今译】真实的话一定是不好听的，好听的话一定不会是真实的。善良的人是不会去争辩的，喜欢争辩的一定不会是善良的人。有智慧的人不见得知识渊博，知识渊博的人不见得有智慧……自然的法则，是对人有利而不会害人的。圣人的原则，就是只去做而不争名利。

【英译】True words are not fine-sounding; fine-sounding words are not true. A good man does not argue; he who argues is not a good man. The wise one does not know many things; he who knows many things is not wise…The Tao of heaven blesses, but does not harm. The way of the sage accomplishes, but does not contend.

《管子》
Guanzi

【简介】《管子》是我国先秦时期的一部鸿篇巨制，内容广博，思想丰富。作者管子（公元前719年至公元前645年），姓管，名夷吾，字仲，是春秋时期法家学派的代表人物，是我国古代重要的政治家、军事家、思想家，他的治国思想和人生哲学集中体现于《管子》一书，这本书对后世产生了深远影响。

【Introduction】 *Guanzi*, an important classic in the pre-Qin period, is characterized by its major length, complex subjects and rich thinking. The author is Guanzi(719~645 BC), with his family name Guan, and given name Yiwu, alias Zhong. Being a representative of Legalism school in the Spring and Autumn period, as well as an important politician, strategist and thinker, his ideology for administrating a country and life philosophy is reflected in his book *Guanzi* which has a profound impact on the later generations.

1. 【原文】必得之事不足赖也，必诺之言不足信也。　　　　　　　　《管子·形势》

   【今译】随便得到的事情靠不住，随便许下的诺言不足信。

   【英译】An easily obtained post is easy to lose; a casually made promise is not worth relying upon.

2. 【原文】不明于象，而欲论材审用，犹绝长以为短，续短以为长。　　《管子·七法》

   【今译】不知道形象变化，而想选拔贤才使用，就好像天下万物可以随心所欲地截长为短、续短为长一样。

   【英译】To select capable people without knowing their characters is like blindly making long things short and short things long, which is to act against the laws of nature.

3. 【原文】不明于则，而欲出号令，犹立朝夕于运均之上。　　　　　　《管子·七法》

   【今译】不明白事物变化的法则，却要发号命令，就好比把日晷立在制作陶器的转轮之上，是无法辨别东西方向的。

   【英译】To issue orders without understanding the laws and regulations is just like erecting a sundial upon a pottery wheel, using which you can never distinguish east from west.

4. 【原文】不为爱人枉其法，故曰法爱于人。　　　　　　　　　　《管子·七法》

   【今译】不因私人感情而枉法，所以说法重于情。

   【英译】The king will never pervert the law owing to personal preference. Ultimately, the law is more important than personal preference.

5. 【原文】不为不可成，不求不可得。　　　　　　　　　　　　　《管子·牧民》

   【今译】不做办不到的事，不求得不到的东西。

   【英译】Never pursue a goal which is unreachable; never seek something that is unattainable.

6. 【原文】不远道里，故能威绝域之民。　　　　　　　　　　　《管子·七法》

   【今译】出奇兵不怕路程遥远，所以能威震远方之敌。

   【英译】Making unexpected military moves in spite of a long distance, thus a far-off enemy may behold one's army in awe.

7. 【原文】不重之结，虽固必解。道之用也，贵其重也。　　　　《管子·形势》

   【今译】随随便便的交情，虽一时稳固后必分裂。交友之道的应用，关键在于郑重。

   【英译】A casual friendship will fall apart sooner or later despite its temporary firmness. The key to the art of making friends lies in seriousness.

8. 【原文】仓廪实则知礼节，衣食足则知荣辱。　　　　　　　　《管子·牧民》

   【今译】先使民富足然后教之礼仪，吃饱穿暖再讲荣耀和耻辱。

   【英译】When the granaries are full, men appreciate rites and obligations; when food and clothing are enough, men have sense of honor and humility.

9. 【原文】沉于乐者洽于忧，厚于味者薄于行，慢于朝者缓于政，害于国家者危于社稷。

   　　　　　　　　　　　　　　　　　　　　　　　　　　　　《管子·中匡》

   【今译】沉溺于享乐会带来忧患，贪图美味就会放松行为修养，怠慢于朝廷就会放松对政事的处理，伤害了国家就会危及政权。

   【英译】Indulging in pleasures will bring about misery, coveting delicacies will weaken selfcultivation, neglecting the imperial court will loosen the reins of government affairs, and lacerating the country will jeopardize state power.

10. 【原文】成功立事，必顺于理义，故不理不胜天下，不义不胜人。　　《管子·七法》

    【今译】事业成功一定要合于理义，所以不合于理就不能战胜天下，不合于义就不能战胜别人。

    【英译】Reason and justice are decisive in achieving success. Therefore, by conforming with reason, the country will be conquered; by conforming with justice, the people will be conquered, and vice versa.

11. 【原文】丹青在山，民知而取之。美珠在渊，民知而取之。是以我有过为，而民毋过命。

《管子·小称》

【今译】山石中有丹青，老百姓知道取而用之。深水中有宝珠，老百姓知道取而用之。我有过错，老百姓一定不会有错误的评价。

【英译】When there is cinnabar in mountain stones, people know and mine it; when there are precious pearls in deep water, people know and obtain them; and when I commit an error, people will know and point it out unerringly.

12. 【原文】道者，一人用之，不闻有余；天下行之，不闻不足。 《管子·白心》

【今译】道用于一人，没听说过有余剩；天下人遵道而行，没听说道不够用。

【英译】It has never been heard that rules and principles are in abundance when applied to an individual; it is also unheard of that they are inadequate as all obey and carry them forward.

13. 【原文】宁过于君子，而毋失于小人。过于君子，其为怨浅；失于小人，其为祸深。

《管子·立政》

【今译】宁肯让君子职位低，也不要让小人处尊位。君子职位低，其埋怨事小；小人处尊位，那可就祸害深远了。

【英译】It is better to have a man of noble character take a low position than to offer a man with a mean disposition a high post, as the former will only bring benign discontent, while the latter will lead to malignant disaster.

14. 【原文】地大国富，人众兵强，此霸王之本也，然而与危亡为邻矣。 《管子·重令》

【今译】土地广博，国家富裕。人口众多，兵力强盛。这是称霸的资本，然而至此也就和国家危亡很接近了。

【英译】A vast landmass, big population, and a strong army, which are the bases of a nation's hegemony, are also the tokens of its approaching collapse.

15. 【原文】多忠少欲，智也，为人臣者之广道也。 《管子·枢言》

【今译】忠诚寡欲，是明智的表现，也是为人臣之正道。

【英译】Having more honesty and less greed, as a wise man has, is the right way for a faithful official to be.

16. 【原文】法出于礼，礼出于治。治、礼，道也。万物待治，礼而后定。 《管子·枢言》

【今译】法出于礼仪，礼仪出于道理。道理和礼仪就是道。天下万物合于道后自然安定。

【英译】Law comes from etiquette. Etiquette originates from reason. Etiquette and reason are the Tao, the absolute principle underlying the universe. Nothing will be in disorder if it follows the principles of the Tao.

17. 【原文】法简而易行，刑审而不犯，事约而易从，求寡而易足。 《管子·桓公问》

【今译】法度简要就会便于实行，量刑慎重就不会再去触犯，政事简约就容易听从，要求少了人们就容易满足。

【英译】Simple laws facilitate execution, whereas prudent execution prevents crime. Concise government policies make more people follow the law of the country, and men with less desire feel more content.

18.【原文】凡兵有大论，必先论其器，论其士，论其将，论其主。　　《管子·参患》

【今译】凡带兵作战先要论辩，论其武器是否精良，其士卒是否勇敢，其主将是否知兵，其国君选将是否得当。

【英译】Several matters should be discussed before fighting a war, including whether the weapons are sharp, the soldiers are brave, the general is resourceful, and whether the king is right in selecting the general.

19.【原文】凡国之亡也，以其长者也。人之自失也，以其所长者也。故善游者死于梁也，善射者死于中野。　　《管子·枢言》

【今译】国家灭亡，往往是因其强盛而好战导致的。人犯错误，往往是因其有过人之长处而骄傲导致的。所以善游泳者死于水，善射者死于战争。

【英译】A nation collapses because it is too powerful and prosperous, and a man makes mistakes for he is wiser than others. Therefore, those drowned in water are always good swimmers and those killed in the battlefield are often excellent archers.

20.【原文】凡言之不可复，行之不可再者，有国者之大禁也。　　《管子·形势解》

【今译】凡是言而无信的话和行而害民的事，圣明之君是不说、不做的。

【英译】A wise and able king will not recant his own words, nor do any deed that will bring harm to his people.

21.【原文】高山仰之，不可极也。深渊度之，不可测也。神明之德，正静其极也。

《管子·九守》

【今译】高山不见顶，渊深不可测。神明之德，无边无际，无处不在。

【英译】Towering mountains and deep waters are beyond measurement. Likewise, the combination of virtue and wisdom is boundless and omnipresent.

22.【原文】规矩者，方圆之正也。虽有巧目利手，不如拙规矩之正方圆也。故巧者能生规矩，不能废规矩而正方圆。　　《管子·法法》

【今译】规矩是校正方圆的器具，虽有目明手巧之人，也不如有个笨规矩校正方形、圆形。所以巧匠能制造出规矩，却不能不用规矩去校正方圆。

【英译】A compass and a carpenter's square are appliances to rectify circulars and squares, which are more valuable than a skilled craftsman. Although it is a skilled craftsman who makes a compass and a carpenter's square, he cannot rectify the circulars and squares without them.

23. 【原文】国虽富，不侈泰，不纵欲；兵虽强，不轻侮诸侯，动众用兵，必为天下正理。

《管子·重令》

【今译】国家虽然富强，也不能奢侈放纵，对欲望不加克制。兵力虽然强盛，也不能随便动用武力欺侮别国，这一定会成为天下正道。

【英译】A powerful and prosperous nation cannot stand for extravagance and indulgence, nor allow itself to satiate its unchecked desires. It must be the principle universally applied that a military power shouldn't bully others at will.

24. 【原文】先王重其宝器而轻其末用，故能为天下。 《管子·枢言》

【今译】先王知道宝和器重要，看轻珠玉，所以能统一天下。

【英译】The former kings conquered and unified the whole country because in their wisdom they knew that treasures and instruments were far more important than pearls and jewels.

25. 【原文】计必先定，而兵出于竟。计未定而兵出于竟，则战之自败，攻之自毁者也。

《管子·参患》

【今译】计谋必须先制定出来，然后军队才可出兵作战。如果计谋未定就出兵作战，战则自败，攻则自毁。

【英译】Strategy should be made before sending troops abroad to fight a war. Otherwise the army will be defeated in a confrontation and destroyed in an offensive attack.

26. 【原文】济于舟者，和于水矣。义于人者，祥其神矣。 《管子·白心》

【今译】水能载舟在于水平静没有波浪，与人和睦相处的人神灵会保佑他幸福吉祥。

【英译】Quiet water floats a boat, as harmonious social relations bring good luck and happiness.

27. 【原文】近者示之以忠信，远者示之以礼仪。行此数年，而民归之如流水。

《管子·霸形》

【今译】以诚恳实在对待国内百姓，以礼仪相待他国民众。这样实行若干年后，远近百姓都会像流水一样归附。

【英译】If, for a good period of years, fellow countrymen are treated with honesty and foreigners with etiquette, the people, from afar or nearby, will come like flowing water and pledge their allegiance to the state.

28. 【原文】君之所审者三：一曰德不当其位，二曰功不当其禄，三曰能不当其官。此三本者，治乱之原也。 《管子·立政》

【今译】国君对官吏考查有三项：其德义是否能加于尊位，其功劳是否能授予重禄，其才能是否能当大官。这三项是国家或治或乱的根源。

【英译】There are three principles for the emperor to use to examine officials. First, if their moral standards match their high position. Second, if their contributions are deserving their salary. Third, if they are equal to their jobs. The law and order of a nation depends on these principles.

29.【原文】立政出令用人道，施爵禄用地道，举大事用天道。　　　　《管子·霸言》

【今译】推行政事要符合人心，使用官员要公平无私，每行大事要应天时。

【英译】Government policies should win the support of people, government officials should be justly appointed, and the great undertaking should follow the order of nature.

30.【原文】凌山阬不待钩梯，历水谷不须舟楫，径于绝地，攻于恃固，独出独入，而莫之能止。　　　　《管子·兵法》

【今译】登山不用钩梯，渡水不用舟楫，过孤绝之地，攻击恃险固守之敌，独来独往，如入无人之境，没有人能阻挡。

【英译】Climbing a mountain without a hook leader, crossing a river without a boat, the army men penetrate the desolate land, attacking the enemies who take the difficulty of access as a defense. They come and go as freely as entering an uninhabited land, all resistance broken.

31.【原文】令重于宝，社稷先于亲戚；法重于民，威权贵于爵禄。　　　　《管子·法法》

【今译】法令重于君主的权力，国家利益重于亲戚的利益，法律重于民意，威势权力比爵位俸禄更重要。

【英译】Decrees outweigh monarchical power, national interests take precedence over family matters, laws outweigh public opinions, and authority should not be defused while offering nobility and salary to those who make contributions to society.

32.【原文】明君不以禄爵私所爱，忠臣不诬能以干爵禄。　　　　《管子·法法》

【今译】贤明之君不用官位俸禄徇私情，忠于君主的臣子不用欺骗手段谋取官职。

【英译】A wise and able monarch will not practise favoritism, and a loyal official will not cheat for promotion.

33.【原文】明主有过，则反之于身；有善，则归之于民。有过而反之身，则身惧。有善而归之民，则民喜。　　　　《管子·小称》

【今译】圣明君主有过错，会反躬自省；有善行，会归之于百姓。有过错时懂得反省，就会因害怕有错而更加注意自身修养；有善行归之于百姓，百姓就会得善而欢喜。

【英译】When something malevolent befalls a state, a capable and virtuous monarch will blame and examine himself; when something benevolent appears, he will give the credit to the common people. Mistakes lead to self-examination, so he will attach great importance to self-cultivation for fear of committing improper acts. The common people will feel joyful and valued if they are credited with doing good deeds for the state.

34. 【原文】目贵明，耳贵聪，心贵智。　　　　　　　　　　　　　　　《管子·九守》

【今译】眼睛重要在于看得明白，耳朵重要在于听得真切，心重要在于思虑得当。

【英译】Eyes are to see clearly, ears to hear accurately and the mind to think wisely and properly.

35. 【原文】其君子上中正而下谄谀，其士民贵武勇而贱得利。　　　　　《管子·五辅》

【今译】君子崇尚正直而鄙视谄谀，士民看重勇武而轻视苟得之利。

【英译】One who has a noble character upholds integrity and despises flattery; one who serves in the military values courage and does not act according to personal interests.

36. 【原文】求必欲得，禁必欲止，令必欲行。求多者其得寡，禁多者其止寡，令多者其行寡。　　　　　　　　　　　　　　　　　　　　　　　　　　《管子·法法》

【今译】追求就一定是想要得到，下禁令就一定是想要禁止，下命令就一定是想要执行。贪求太多得到的反而会少，禁令太多服从的人反而会少，号令太多能执行的反而会少。

【英译】It is certain that pursuit of something is to gain it, a prohibition to prevent something happening, and a decree made in the expectation of it being carried out effectively. However, greater pursuits result in little gain, too many prohibitions bring about more violations, and additional decrees lead to less compliance.

37. 【原文】日月不明，天不易也。山高而不见，地不易也。言而不可复者，居不言也。行而不可再者，君不行也。　　　　　　　　　　　　　　　　　　《管子·形势》

【今译】日月不明，是因为有云气遮蔽。山高看不见，是因为地面不平而险阻挡。不能兑现的话，明主不说。不正当的行为，明主不做。

【英译】A cloudy and foggy day makes both the sun and the moon look dim. The rugged land keeps the mountains from view. A wise monarch should not promise something out of his reach, or carry out deeds considered unjust.

38. 【原文】山林虽广，草木虽美，禁发必有时。国虽充盛，金玉虽多，宫室必有度。

《管子·八观》

【今译】山林虽然广阔，草木虽然茂盛，但砍伐一定要有时间限制。国家虽然富裕，金玉宝物虽多，但建造宫室一定要有限度。

【英译】Abundance of forest and vastness of grassland do not grant the right to unlimited exploitation; richness in the treasure of a nation does not automatically allow for the construction of an excessively lavish palace.

39. 【原文】善者之为兵也，使敌若据虚，若搏景。 《管子·兵法》

 【今译】善于用兵的人指挥军队，总能来无影，去无踪，使敌人抓不住，打不着，看不见。

 【英译】An army comes and goes without a trace under the leadership of a good commander. In this way, the enemy will be unable to locate, catch, or attack them.

40. 【原文】上无固植，下有疑心。 《管子·法法》

 【今译】国君没有坚定的意志，臣下就怀疑不定。

 【英译】It is a general rule that officials will be oversensitive and vacillating if the monarch isn't resolute and steadfast.

41. 【原文】少而习焉，其心安焉，不见异物而迁焉。 《管子·小匡》

 【今译】少年学习，心思安定，不会见异思迁。

 【英译】From a young age a boy starts to study, and he will thus be constant in his pursuit and immune to various temptations.

42. 【原文】审其所好恶，则其长短可知也；观其交游，则其贤不肖可察也。

 《管子·权修》

 【今译】仔细观察他的好恶，就知道他的长处和不足。审视他交游的对象，就知道他有无才能。

 【英译】You can learn someone's merits and failings by looking carefully at their likes and dislikes, and measure someone's competency by examining their friends.

43. 【原文】收天下之豪杰，有天下之骏雄，故举之如飞鸟，动之如雷电，发之如风雨，莫当其前，莫害其后，独出独入，莫敢禁圉。 《管子·七发》

 【今译】集合天下豪杰之士和良马组成军队，起兵轻捷如飞鸟，动之以雷霆万钧之势，行军神速如急风暴雨，使敌人闻风丧胆，前不敢挡，后不敢追，如入无人之境，敌人不能抵御。

 【英译】The army, assembling heroic men and well-bred horses, raises troops with the spry lightness of a flying bird, operates with the great momentum of a thunderbolt, marches with the awesome quickness of a storm, and has no barriers before it or troops in pursuit behind it, as the enemies will become terror-stricken on hearing of its coming, and it shall breaks through all resistance like it is entering an uninhabited land.

44. 【原文】授事以能，则人上功。 《管子·问第》

 【今译】任用有才能的人，人们就会崇尚建功立业。

 【英译】Assigning a capable person to a post ensures success.

45. 【原文】数战则士罢，数胜则君骄。 《管子·兵法》

 【今译】连续作战士兵一定疲惫，数次胜利君主必然骄傲。

【英译】The soldiers must be tired of constant war, and the monarch must be conceited after multiple victories.

46.【原文】所谓德者，先之之谓也。故德莫如先，应适莫如后。　　《管子·枢言》

【今译】所谓德，就是率先施德于民的意思。所以施德于民越早越好，而与敌人交战还是后发制人的好。

【英译】The virtuous will show kindness to people at the first opportunity, however, it is better to gain mastery of a battle by striking only after the enemy has struck.

47.【原文】天不变其常，地不易其则，春秋冬夏不更其节，古今一也。　《管子·形势》

【今译】天不改变它的常规，地不改变它的法则，四季不改变它的节令，自古至今，始终不变。

【英译】The law of heaven will never change. The earth prospers under its rule. Under it the four seasons have their own natural phenomena. This has been a natural law unchanged since ancient times.

48.【原文】天道之极，远者自亲；人事之起，近亲造怨。　　《管子·形势》

【今译】完全按自然规律办事，疏远的人也会亲近；人与人之间私心杂念一旦萌生，即使亲近的人也会生怨。

【英译】Strangers will establish harmony among themselves if the law of nature is followed well; even intimates will hold a grudge against each other if the idea for pursuing the personal interests occurs to them.

49.【原文】天时不祥，则有水旱；地道不宜，则有饥馑；人道不顺，则有祸乱。

《管子·五辅》

【今译】天时不吉祥，就会有水旱之灾；地利不适宜，庄稼无收就会有饥荒发生；人道不和顺，就会发生祸乱。

【英译】When the meteorological pattern is irregular, floods and droughts occur. When the condition of the earth is unfit, poor harvests and famines befall. When moral standards are decadent, calamities and scourges arise.

50.【原文】天下不患无臣，患无君以使之。天下不患无财，患无人以分之。

《管子·牧民》

【今译】天下不愁没有能做官的人，只愁没有明君来差使他们。天下不愁没有财富，只愁没有人来管理财富。

【英译】There is no lack of capable officials, just the want of a monarch to make good use of them. There is no lack of money, just the want of a virtuous man to manage it.

51.【原文】天下无私爱也，无私憎也，为善者有福，为不善者有祸。　《管子·枢言》

【今译】天道公正无私没有偏爱，也没有偏恶，行善得福，行恶得祸。

【英译】The rule of nature is just and disinterested, without partiality or prejudice. Good shall be rewarded with good, and evil with evil.

52.【原文】天下者，无常乱，无常治。　　　　　　　　　　《管子·小称》

【今译】天下形势不会一直混乱，也不会一直清明安定。

【英译】The land under heaven will never be in constant chaos or in everlasting order.

53.【原文】听之术，曰：勿望而距，勿望而许。许之则失守，距之则闭塞。

《管子·九守》

【今译】听取意见的方法就是听后必须审察，不可望风而拒绝或应允。盲目应允就会失去原则，盲目拒绝就会阻塞言路。

【英译】The way to take advice is to examine it after listening to someone. One should not accept or reject it hastily. A person's principles will be violated if they accept advice blindly; however, no one will give advice to one who readily ignores other's opinions.

54.【原文】万物之于人也，无私近也，无私远也，巧者有余，而拙者不足。《管子·形势》

【今译】天下万物对于人都是公平的，无远无近，巧者用之有余，拙者用之不足。

【英译】Nothing in the world is in shortage or in abundance. A skillful person can find a thing in abundance while an inept man finds it in shortage.

55.【原文】乌集之交，初虽相驩，后必相咄。故曰：乌集之交，虽善不亲。

《管子·形势解》

【今译】像乌鸦聚集一样地交往，开始虽也亲密，终必离数。所以说，乌集之交，看起来虽然友好但并不亲密。

【英译】Relations developed in a motley crowd may be intimate at first, but will finally cease to exist. Crows that flock together may seem close but will never form long friendship.

56.【原文】无土而欲富者忧，无德而欲王者危，施薄而求厚者孤。　《管子·霸言》

【今译】没有土地而想富裕的人会忧愁，无德却想称霸天下的人是危险的，给予人的少而求回报多的人只会孤独无助。

【英译】A man who has no land, yet wants to be rich, is sad; a man who has no virtue, yet wants to be king, is dangerous; a man who has little commitment, yet wants to be rewarded, is lonely and helpless.

57.【原文】小谨者不大立，訾食者不肥体。　　　　　　　　　《管子·形势》

【今译】谨小慎微的人难有大志，好比厌食的人吃不胖一样。

【英译】An overcautious person seldom has lofty aspirations, as a man suffering from anorexia cannot gain weight.

58. 【原文】孝弟者，仁之祖也。忠信者，交之庆也。 《管子·戒第》

【今译】孝敬父母、敬爱兄长是仁爱的根本。诚恳实在，才能交到好朋友。

【英译】Finally piety is the origin of benevolence, as only a faithful and steadfast person can make a good friend.

59. 【原文】邪莫如蚤禁之。 《管子·法法》

【今译】歪门邪道不如早禁止。

【英译】It is better to put an end to evil thoughts and deeds in their gestational period.

60. 【原文】邪行亡乎体，违言不存口，静然定生，圣也。 《管子·戒第》

【今译】不做不正当的事，不说不合情理的话，无欲则生命安定，这样的人就是圣人啊。

【英译】The man who leads a peaceful life, free of desires, and without committing or uttering improper deeds and words, is a saint.

61. 【原文】心有欲者，物过而目不见，声至而耳不闻也。故曰：上离其道，下失其事。 《管子·心术上》

【今译】心有贪欲，就会万物在眼前却看不见，声音在耳边却听不见。所以说，心一旦离开正道，其他器官就不能主事了。

【英译】A greedy man cannot see or hear clearly. Therefore, if a man's mind is warped, the rest of his body will not function correctly.

62. 【原文】信之者仁也，不可欺者智也。既智且仁，是谓成人。 《管子·枢言》

【今译】诚信就是仁，不受欺骗就是有智慧。如果能做到既有智慧又诚信，也就算是个完人了。

【英译】Honesty and credit are benevolence. And a wise man will not be cheated. If a man is wise, as well as creditable, he can be said to be the perfect man.

63. 【原文】刑罚不足以畏其意，杀戮不足以服其心。 《管子·牧民》

【今译】刑罚不能改变百姓的意愿，杀戮也不能使百姓心服。

【英译】Punishments cannot change the will of the common people, and executions will not lead to gaining superiority over them either.

64. 【原文】形不正者德不来，中不精者心不治。 《管子·心术下》

【今译】外形不端正，内心一定没有德行，内心不真诚就不会安定。

【英译】A person with a wretched appearance must be evil inside; without honesty and sincerity, one's mind could not be in peace.

65. 【原文】一年之计，莫如树谷；十年之计，莫如树木；终身之计，莫如树人。

《管子·权修》

【今译】为一年算计，不如种植五谷；为十年算计，不如种植树木；为一辈子算计，不如培养人才。

【英译】When planning for a year, plant cereals. When planning for a decade, plant trees. When planning for life, train and educate the people.

66.【原文】一期之师，十年之蓄积殚。一战之费，累代之功尽。　　　　《管子·参患》

【今译】军队打一次战，能耗费国家十年积蓄。举国一战，能耗尽几代人的功绩。

【英译】A troop of soldiers fighting a war will cost ten years of national savings; a nation fighting a war will have the cost of ruining the merits and achievements made by several generations.

67.【原文】早知敌而独行，有蓄积则久而不匮，器械巧则伐而不费，赏罚明则勇士劝也。

《管子·兵法》

【今译】提前掌握敌情就能战无不胜；财物储备多就能久战而不匮乏；武器精良就能取胜快，不浪费时间；赏罚分明就能让战士得到最好的勉励。

【英译】There is no war that cannot be won if an army knows much about its enemy in advance; it will not be exhausted because financial and material supply is guaranteed. Fine weapons will accelerate its victory, and clear rewards and punishments will provide the best boost to morale.

68.【原文】朝忘其事，夕失其功。邪气袭内，正色乃衰。　　　　《管子·形势》

【今译】早晨不勉力务进，晚上就没有成果。不正之气侵入内心，面容就会正气衰退。

【英译】One who has accomplished nothing at the end of the day must not have worked hard during the day. A man will have a wretched appearance if he is evil and wicked inside.

69.【原文】召远在修近，闭祸在除怨，修长在乎任贤，安高在乎同利。

《管子·版法》

【今译】与近处的百姓修好，远处的民众就会来投奔。消除怨恨就会不生祸乱。任用有才能的人，国家就能长治久安。能与百姓同享利益，君主才会安泰。

【英译】If one gets along well with the people around him, those who live afar will wish to go to him for shelter. If resentment is appeased, turmoil will not arise. If a monarch governs with capable officials, long-term peace and the stability of the nation will be ensured, and if he is of one mind with the people, his authority will be firm and steady.

70.【原文】政之所兴，在顺民心；政之所废，在逆民心。　　　　《管子·牧民》

【今译】政令通达，在于顺应民心；政令废止，在于不能顺应民心。

【英译】A government decree that meets the aspirations of the common people will be implemented effectively; otherwise, it will be of no avail.

71. 【原文】治国之道，必先富民，民富则易治也，民贫则难治也。 　　《管子·治国》

【今译】治国之道，必先使百姓富裕。百姓富裕就容易治理，百姓贫穷就难以治理。

【英译】Enriching the people is the prerequisite to administrate a nation. It is easy to establish order if the common people are rich, whereas if they are poor, it is a much harder task.

72. 【原文】众若时雨，寡若飘风，一之终也。 　　《管子·兵法》

【今译】我军数倍于敌人时就用包围诱降的办法瓦解他们，我军少于敌人时就用奇兵突袭的战术制服他们。人多能战胜敌人，人少能战胜敌人，这是以道用兵的最高境界。

【英译】To besiege the enemies and lure them into surrender when overwhelming in number, to launch a surprise attack and triumph over the enemies when few in number, to be able to defeat the enemies under both conditions is the highest achievement of a commander of troops.

73. 【原文】壮者无怠，老者无偷，顺天之道，必以善终者也。 　　《管子·中匡》

【今译】壮年时不懒惰，老年时不苟且，行事遵循天道，就一定会终享天年的。

【英译】Be neither slothful in the meridian of one's life, nor drift along in one's old age, by following these laws of nature one will live a full and tranquil life.

74. 【原文】追亡逐遁若飘风，击刺若雷电。绝地不守，恃固不拔。 　　《管子·兵法》

【今译】追逐逃敌像疾风一样快，攻击敌人如万钧雷霆一样猛烈。不据守孤绝之地，不攻打固守之敌。

【英译】An army should chase the fleeing enemies as quickly as the wind, and attack the enemies as fiercely as a thunderbolt. Never defend an isolated position, and never launch an attack on an impregnable fortress.

《论语》
The Analects of Confucius

【简介】《论语》是一部语录体散文集，成书于战国初期，由孔子弟子编纂而成，主要记载孔子及其弟子的言行，较为集中地反映了孔子的思想。南宋时期（1127 年至 1279 年），朱熹将它和《孟子》《大学》《中庸》合称为"四书"。孔子（公元前 551 年 9 月 28 日至公元前 479 年 4 月 11 日），名丘，字仲尼，春秋时期鲁国人，著名的思想家、教育家、政治家，儒家学派的创始人。

【Introduction】 *The Analects of Confucius* reflecting Confucian doctrine, a record of words and deeds about Confucius and his disciples, was written in the early phase of the Warring States period (c.475~221 BC). In Southern Song dynasty(1127~1279), Zhu Xi(1130~1200, the later epitome of Confucian school) regarded *The Analects of Confucius, Mencius, The Great Learning* and *The Doctrine of the Mean* as The Four Books. Confucius(c.551~479 BC) is a native of Lu in the Spring and Autumn period with his family name Kong, surname Qiu, alias Zhongni. As a great thinker, educator and statesman, he is the founder of Confucian school.

1. 【原文】子曰："学而时习之，不亦说乎？有朋自远方来，不亦乐乎？人不知而不愠，不亦君子乎？"
《论语·学而》

   【今译】孔子说："将学到的东西不断地用于实践不是一件很开心的事吗？有志同道合的朋友从远方来看望自己难道不会很快乐吗？自己的学识、抱负没有人认可或知道而不心存怨恨，这难道不是君子吗？"

   【英译】The Master said, "Is it not a pleasure, having learned something, to try it out at due intervals? Is it not a joy to have friends come from afar? Is it not gentlemanly not to take offence when others fail to appreciate your abilities?"

2. 【原文】有子曰："其为人也孝弟，而好犯上者，鲜矣；不好犯上，而好作乱者，未之有也。君子务本，本立而道生。孝弟也者，其为仁之本与！"
《论语·学而》

   【今译】有子说："一个人很孝顺父母而且疼爱自己的兄弟姐妹，却又经常对别的长辈或地位比自己高的人不恭敬，这样的人是很少存在的；不会对比自己年长的人或地位高的人不恭，却又经常胡作非为的人我从来没有见过。君子专心致力于根本的事务，基础建立了，治国做人的原则也就有了。孝顺父母，敬爱兄长，这就是仁的根本啊！"

   【英译】Yu Tzu said, "It is rare for a man whose character is such that he is good as a son and obedient as a young man to have the inclination to transgress against his superiors; it is unheard of for one who has no such inclination to be inclined to start a rebellion. The gentleman devotes his efforts to the roots, for once the roots are established, the way will grow therefrom. Being good as a son and obedient as a young man is, perhaps, the root of a man's character."

3. 【原文】曾子曰："吾日三省吾身：为人谋而不忠乎？与朋友交而不信乎？传不习乎？"
《论语·学而》

   【今译】曾子说："我每天都会反省自己很多次：帮别人做事是否尽心尽力？与朋友交往

有没有不守信用？学到的知识是否不断温习或应用起来？"

【英译】Tseng Tzu said, "Every day I examine myself on three counts. In what I have undertaken on another's behalf, have I failed to do my best? In my dealings with my friends, have I failed to be trustworthy in what I say? Have I passed on to others anything that I have not tried out myself?"

4. 【原文】子曰："道千乘之国，敬事而信，节用而爱人，使民以时。" 《论语·学而》

【今译】孔子说："治理大国的人应该做到：做事兢兢业业，信守承诺，认真严谨地处理国家政事，节约财政开支，友爱同僚，役使民众而不误他们的农时。"

【英译】The Master said, "In guiding a state of a thousand chariots, approach your duties with reverence and be trustworthy in what you say, avoid excesses in expenditure and love your fellow men, employ the labour of the common people only in the right seasons."

5. 【原文】子曰："弟子，入则孝，出则悌，谨而信，泛爱众，而亲仁。行有余力，则以学文。" 《论语·学而》

【今译】孔子说："年轻人在家要孝父母，出门要敬爱兄长，为人处世谨慎而又言而有信，尊敬、爱护每一个人，亲近有仁德的人。做到了这些并且有余力就可以继续学习各种文化知识。"

【英译】The Master said, "A young man should be a good son at home and an obedient young man abroad, sparing of speech but trustworthy in what he says, and should love the multitude at large but cultivate the friendship of his fellow men. If he has any energy to spare from such action, let him devote it to making himself cultivated."

6. 【原文】子夏曰："贤贤、易色；事父母，能竭其力；事君，能致其身；与朋友交，言而有信。虽曰未学，吾必谓之学矣。" 《论语·学而》

【今译】子夏说："尊敬贤德的人并不断向他们学习，改正自己错误的做法；侍奉父母要尽心尽力，竭尽自己的力量；服务君王能全身心地奉献；与朋友交往重诺守义，言而有信。即使这样的人没有读过一天书，我一定说他是很有学问的。"

【英译】Tzu-hisa said, "I would grant that a man has received instruction who appreciates men of excellence where other men appreciate beautiful women, who exerts himself to the utmost in the service of his parents and offers his person to the service of his lord, and who, in his dealings with his friends, is trustworthy in what he says, even though he may say that he has never been taught."

7. 【原文】子曰："君子不重，则不威；学则不固。主忠信。无友不如己者，过，则勿惮改。" 《论语·学而》

【今译】孔子说："一个人不自重自爱就不会有威严，不断学习才不会鄙陋。恪守忠信，与志同道合的人做朋友，有了过错要去改正，不要害怕改变。"

【英译】The Master said, "A gentleman who lacks gravity does not inspire awe. A gentleman who studies is unlikely to be inflexible. Make it your guiding principle to do your best for others and to be trustworthy in what you say. Do not accept as friend anyone who is not so good as you. When you make a mistake, do not be afraid of mending your ways."

8.【原文】子禽问于子贡曰:"夫子至于是邦也,必闻其政,求之与?抑与之与?"子贡曰:"夫子温、良、恭、俭、让以得之。夫子之求之也,其诸异乎人之求之与?"

《论语·学而》

【今译】子禽向子贡请教问题:"老师(孔子)每到一个国家就总是能知道这个国家的政令、政风,这是老师去请求得来的呢?还是有人主动告诉他呢?"子贡回答说:"老师温良如玉,恭敬俭朴谦让,所以才会有资格知道这些事。老师得到的方法大概与别人的方法不同吧!"

【英译】Tzu-ch'in asked Tzu-kung, "When the Master arrives in a state, he invariably gets to know about its government. Does he seek this information? Or is it given to him?" Tzu-kung said, "The Master gets it through being cordial, good, respectful, frugal and deferential. The way the Master seeks it is, perhaps, different from the way other men seek it."

9.【原文】子曰:"父在,观其志;父没,观其行;三年无改于父之道,可谓孝矣。"

《论语·学而》

【今译】孔子说:"父亲在世的时候,应该观察儿子的思想、志向;父亲去世以后,应该观察儿子的所作所为。如果过了很长的一段时间儿子都没有改变当时好的作为,就可以说他是很孝顺的了。"

【英译】The Master said, "Observe what a man has in mind to do when his father is living, and then observe what he does when his father is dead. If, for three years, he makes no change to his father's ways, he can be said to be a good son."

10.【原文】有子曰:"礼之用,和为贵。先王之道,斯为美,小人出之。有所不行,知和而和,不以礼节之,亦不可行也。"

《论语·学而》

【今译】有子说:"礼的应用,以和谐为关键。先代圣王的治国方法中最可贵的地方就在于他们做所有的事都以此为出发点。如果不能做到这一点,只为求和谐的目的而去做,但不以'礼'的精髓制约行为,也是行不通的。"

【英译】Yu Tzu said, "Of the things brought about by the rites, harmony is the most valuable. Of the ways of the former kings, this is the most beautiful, and is followed alike in matters great and small. Yet this will not always work. To aim always at harmony without regulating it by the rites simply because one knows only about harmony will not, in fact, work."

11.【原文】有子曰:"信近于义,言可复也。恭近于礼,远耻辱也。因不失其亲,亦可宗也。"
《论语·学而》

【今译】有子说:"信守承诺的行为合乎于'义',这样的言辞才能够被履行;态度容貌的庄重矜持要符合于礼,这样的行为才不至于遭受侮辱;所依靠的人都是关系亲密的、值得依靠的人,这样才可靠。"

【英译】Yu Tzu said, "To be trustworthy in word is close to being moral in that it enables one's words to be repeated. To be respectful is close to being observant of the rites in that it enables one to stay clear of disgrace and insult. If, in promoting good relationship with relatives by marriage, a man manages not to lose the good will of his own kinsmen, he is worthy of being looked up to as the head of the clan."

12.【原文】子曰:"君子食无求饱,居无求安,敏于事而慎于言,就有道而正焉,可谓好学也已。"
《论语·学而》

【今译】孔子说:"君子(代指一般有德行的人)在饮食上不求饱足,果腹即可;住所上不求安逸,栖身则已;对事情有敏锐的看法而又慎于言辞,向有道德的人看齐并不断端正自己的行为,这样就算是好学的人了。"

【英译】The Master said, "The gentleman seeks neither a full belly nor a comfortable home. He is quick in action but cautious in speech. He goes to men possessed of the way to be put right. Such a man can be described as eager to learn."

13.【原文】子贡曰:"贫而无谄,富而无骄,何如?"子曰:"可也,未若贫而乐,富而好礼者也。"子贡曰:"《诗》云,'如切如磋,如琢如磨。'其斯之谓与?"子曰:"赐也,始可与言《诗》已矣,告诸往而知来者。"
《论语·学而》

【今译】子贡说:"没钱而不谄媚别人,有钱而不骄奢待人,怎么样呀?"孔子说:"这样的人也算是不错了,但是不如虽然贫穷却乐观地生活、富贵而谦恭好礼的人呀!"子贡说:"《诗经》讲,要像对待骨、角、象牙、玉石一样,切磋它,琢磨它,这就是做人或做学问的方法吧?"孔子赞叹道:"赐啊!已经可以和你讲解《诗经》了,你已能从我讲的过去的事情中领会到另外没有说到的意思了。"

【英译】Tzu-kung said, "'Poor without being obsequious, wealthy without being arrogant.' What do you think of this saying?" The Master said, "That will do, but better still 'poor yet delighting in the way, wealthy yet observant of the rites.'" Tzu-kung said, "The *Odes* say, 'Like bone cut, like horn polished, like jade carved, like stone ground.' Is it not what you have said a case in point?" The Master said, "Ssu, only with a man like you can one discuss the *Odes*. Tell such a man something and he can see its relevance to what he has not been told."

14.【原文】子曰:"不患人之不己知,患不知人也。"
《论语·学而》

【今译】孔子说:"不担心别人不知道自己,而担心自己不了解别人啊!"

【英译】The Master said, "It is not the failure of others to appreciate your abilities that should trouble you, but rather your failure to appreciate theirs."

15. 【原文】子曰:"为政以德,譬如北辰,居其所而众星共之。"　　　　《论语·为政》

    【今译】孔子说:"如果君王以'德'治理国家,那就会像北极星一样,安居在自己的位置而其余众星有序地环绕在它的周围(随它的方向前进)。"

    【英译】The Master said, "The rule of virtue can be compared to the Pole Star which commands the homage of the multitude of stars without leaving its place."

16. 【原文】子曰:"《诗》三百,一言以蔽之,曰:'思无邪。'"　　　　《论语·为政》

    【今译】孔子说:"《诗经》的全部内容用一句话来概括就是:'思想纯正'。"

    【英译】The Master said, "The *Odes* are three hundred in number. They can be summed up in one phrase—swerving not from the right path."

17. 【原文】子曰:"道之以政,齐之以刑,民免而无耻;道之以德,齐之以礼,有耻且格。"
    　　　　　　　　　　　　　　　　　　　　　　　　　　　　　《论语·为政》

    【今译】孔子说:"如果用行政命令来训导民众,用严刑酷法来整束民众,民众只会千方百计避免获罪而丧失廉耻之心;如果用道德引导民众,用礼仪约束民众,民众就会有羞耻之心并且努力(改正自己)以达到要求。"

    【英译】The Master said, "Guide them by edicts, keep them in line with punishments, and the common people will stay out of trouble but will have no sense of shame. Guide them by virtue, keep them in line with the rites, and they will, besides having a sense of shame, reform themselves."

18. 【原文】子曰:"吾十有五而志于学,三十而立,四十而不惑,五十而知天命,六十而耳顺,七十而从心所欲,不逾矩。"　　　　　　　　　　　　《论语·为政》

    【今译】孔子说:"我十五岁的时候立下了学习的志向,三十岁时说话、做事有了把握,四十岁时掌握了知识开始不因外界事物困惑,五十岁时知晓天命,六十岁时对不利于自己的意见也会正确对待,七十岁以后则能行动都随自己的心意而又不会越过世俗规矩。"

    【英译】The Master said, "At fifteen I set my heart on learning; at thirty I took my stand; at forty I came to be free from doubts; at fifty I understood the decree of heaven; at sixty my ear was attuned; at seventy I followed my heart's desire without overstepping the line."

19. 【原文】孟武伯问孝。子曰:"父母唯其疾之忧。"　　　　　　　　《论语·为政》

    【今译】孟武伯问孔子什么是"孝"。孔子回答说:"孝顺父母就是要(时刻)关心他们的身体,为他们的疾病担忧。"

    【英译】Meng Wu Po asked about being filial. The Master said, "Give your father and mother no other cause for anxiety than illness."

20. 【原文】子夏问孝，子曰："色难。" 《论语·为政》

【今译】子夏问孔子什么是"孝"。孔子说："要做到和颜悦色、始终恭敬最不容易。"

【英译】Tzu-hsia asked about being filial. The Master said, "What is difficult to manage is the expression on one's face."

21. 【原文】子曰："视其所以，观其所由，察其所安。人焉廋哉？人焉廋哉？" 《论语·为政》

【今译】孔子说："（要考察一个人）就要看他所做过的事情，观察他曾经的经历，看他的秉性涵养，这样一个人怎么能掩藏起自己来呢？怎么能掩藏起自己来呢？"

【英译】The Master said, "Look at the means a man employs, observe the path he takes and examine where he feels at home. In what way is a man's true character hidden from view? In what way is a man's true character hidden from view?"

22. 【原文】子曰："温故而知新，可以为师矣。" 《论语·为政》

【今译】孔子说："不断温习以前学到的知识，不断从中阐发出新的体会，这样的人可以做老师了。"

【英译】The Master said, "A man is worthy of being a teacher who gets to know what is new by keeping fresh in his mind what he is already familiar with."

23. 【原文】子曰："君子不器。" 《论语·为政》

【今译】孔子说："君子不会像器皿一样只具备某一方面的才能。"

【英译】The master said, "The gentleman is no vessel."

24. 【原文】子贡问君子。子曰："先行其言而后从之。" 《论语·为政》

【今译】子贡问孔子怎样做一个君子。孔子说："对于要说的话，先将它付诸行动，然后再将它说出来（这样才是君子）。"

【英译】Tzu-kung asked about the gentleman. The Master said, "He puts his words into action before allowing his words to follow his action."

25. 【原文】子曰："君子周而不比，小人比而不周。" 《论语·为政》

【今译】孔子说："君子与人相处合群而不勾结，小人则是与人勾结而不合群。"

【英译】The Master said, "The gentleman enters into associations but not cliques; the small man enters into cliques but not associations."

26. 【原文】子曰："学而不思则罔，思而不学则殆。" 《论语·为政》

【今译】孔子说："单纯学习知识但不去思索就会茫然、迷惑，只是不断空想但不学习实践就会迷惑、茫然。"

【英译】The Master said, "If one learns from others but does not think, one will be bewildered.

If, on the other hand, one thinks but does not learn from others, one will be in peril."

27. 【原文】子曰:"攻乎异端,斯害也已。" 《论语·为政》

   【今译】孔子说:"(不讲道理地)攻击反对不同于己的言论或事物,这种行为也是错误的。"

   【英译】The Master said, "To attack a task from the wrong end can do nothing but harm."

28. 【原文】子曰:"由!诲女知之乎?知之为知之,不知为不知,是知也。"
   《论语·为政》

   【今译】孔子说:"由啊,我教导你的你明白吗?对一件事,知道就是知道,不知道就是不知道,这就是有智慧啊。"

   【英译】The Master said, "Yu, shall I tell you what it is to know. To say you know when you know, and to say you do not when you do not, and that is knowledge."

29. 【原文】子张学干禄。子曰:"多闻阙疑,慎言其余,则寡尤;多见阙殆,慎行其余,则寡悔。言寡尤,行寡悔,禄在其中矣。" 《论语·为政》

   【今译】子张问怎样求取官职。孔子回答说:"多听取别人的意见,有疑问的就先将它搁置在一边,对有把握的事也不要轻易地讨论,这样说话就会少犯错误;遇到事情要多观察,有怀疑的就先不做,对有把握的事也要谨慎地去处理,这样做事就不会有太多悔恨。做到了少说错话,少做错事,官职俸禄自然就能得到。"

   【英译】Tzu-chang was studying with an eye to an official career. The Master said, "Use your ears widely but leave out what is doubtful. Repeat the rest with caution and you will make few mistakes. Use your eyes widely and leave out what is hazardous. Put the rest into practice with caution and you will have few regrets. When in your speech you make few mistakes and in your action you have few regrets, an official career will follow as a matter of course."

30. 【原文】哀公问曰:"何为则民服?"孔子对曰:"举直错诸枉,则民服;举枉错诸直,则民不服。" 《论语·为政》

   【今译】哀公问孔子:"怎样做才能使民众臣服?"孔子回答说:"选拔任用正直公平的人,把不正直的人放置一旁,那么民众就会臣服;任用不正直的人而将正直无私的人放置不予任用,则民众不会臣服。"

   【英译】Duke Ai asked, "What must I do before the common people will look up to me?" Confucius answered, "Raise the straight and set them over the crooked and the common people will look up to you. Raise the crooked and set them over the straight and the common people will not look up to you."

31. 【原文】季康子问:"使民敬、忠以劝,如之何?"子曰:"临之以庄,则敬;孝慈,

则忠；举善而教不能，则劝。"   《论语·为政》

【今译】季康子问孔子："要使民众恭敬、忠厚，并且自勉努力，应该怎样做呢？"孔子说："对待民众庄重威严，他们就会态度恭敬；通过自己的行为引导百姓孝敬父母，慈爱兄弟，则民风忠厚；提拔良善的人而教导能力差的人，人们就会自勉努力了。"

【英译】Chi K'ang Tzu asked, "How can one inculcate in common people the virtue of reverence, of doing their best and of enthusiasm?" The Master said, "Rule over them with dignity and they will be reverent; treat them with kindness and they will do their best; raise the good and instruct those who are backward and they will be imbued with enthusiasm."

32.【原文】子曰："人而无信，不知其可也。"   《论语·为政》

【今译】孔子说："一个人做事没有信誉，会让人不知道他到底想做什么，让人无所适从。"

【英译】The Master said, "I do not see how a man can be acceptable who is untrustworthy in word."

33.【原文】子曰："其非鬼而祭之，谄也。见义不为，无勇也。"

《论语·为政》

【今译】孔子说："不是自己家的祖先而去祭祀他，这是谄媚的行为，见到应该做的事而不做就是没有勇气。"

【英译】The Master said, "To offer sacrifice to the spirit of an ancestor not one's own is obsequious. Faced with what is right, to leave it undone shows a lack of courage."

34.【原文】孔子谓季氏："八佾舞于庭，是可忍也，孰不可忍也？"   《论语·八佾》

【今译】孔子评论季平子说："季家用违反礼仪的八佾在自家庭院里演出，这种事情都被容忍做出来了，还有什么事做不出来呢？"

【英译】Confucius said of the Chi Family, "They use eight rows of eight dancers each to perform in their courtyard. If this can be tolerated, what cannot be tolerated?"

35.【原文】子曰："人而不仁，如礼何？人而不仁，如乐何？"   《论语·八佾》

【今译】孔子说："为人没有仁德，他要怎样实行礼制呢？为人没有仁德，他要怎样运用乐制呢？"

【英译】The Master said, "What can a man do with the rites who is not benevolent?What can a man do with music who is not benevolent?"

36.【原文】林放问礼之本。子曰："大哉问！礼，与其奢也，宁俭；丧，与其易也，宁戚。"

《论语·八佾》

【今译】林放向孔子询问"礼"的根本。孔子回答说："这是多么重要的问题呀！礼仪，与其奢侈宁愿俭朴；丧礼，与其仪式铺张不如内心悲戚。"

【英译】Lin Fang asked about the basis of the rites. The Master said, "A noble question indeed! With the rites, it is better to err on the side of frugality than on the side of extravagance; in mourning, it is better to err on the side of grief than on the side of formality."

37.【原文】子曰："君子无所争，必也射乎！揖让而升，下而饮，其争也君子。"

《论语·八佾》

【今译】孔子说："君子没有什么争强好胜的心，如果有的话，那就在射箭比赛上表现最明显了。开始比赛时，先拱手行礼以示尊敬，相互礼让后上场，射完箭又相互作揖，再退下来一起喝酒。这种争的方式也是君子的做法。"

【英译】The Master said, "There is no contention between gentlemen. The nearest to it is, perhaps, archery. In archery they bow and make way for one another as they go up and on coming down they drink together. Even the way they contend is gentlemanly."

38.【原文】祭如在，祭神如神在。子曰："吾不与祭，如不祭。"   《论语·八佾》

【今译】祭祀祖先就要像祖宗在自己面前一样恭敬，祭祀神灵就要像真正面对神灵一样虔诚。孔子说："如果我没有全心投入到祭祀中去，不如不去祭祀。"

【英译】"Sacrifice as if present" is taken to mean "sacrifice to the gods as if the gods were present." The Master, however, said, "Unless I take part in a sacrifice, it is as if I did not sacrifice."

39.【原文】子曰："获罪于天，无所祷也。"   《论语·八佾》

【今译】孔子说："当所做的事为天理难容时，无论向谁祈祷都没有用。"

【英译】The Master said, "When you have offended against heaven, there is nowhere you can turn to in your prayers."

40.【原文】子贡欲去告朔之饩羊。子曰："赐也！尔爱其羊，我爱其礼。"

《论语·八佾》

【今译】子贡想要取消每月初一祭祀时用的活羊。孔子知道后说："赐啊！你舍不得你的羊，但我舍不得的是我的礼呀。"

【英译】Tzu-kung wanted to do away with the sacrificial sheep at the announcement of the new moon. The Master said, "Ssu, you are loath to part with the price of the sheep, but I am loath to see the disappearance of the rite."

41.【原文】子曰："事君尽礼，人以为谄也。"   《论语·八佾》

【今译】孔子说："侍奉君王一切都按照礼制的要求去做，别人却以为是在向君主献媚。"

【英译】The Master said, "You will be looked upon as obsequious by others if you observe every detail of the rites in serving your lord."

42. 【原文】孔子对曰:"君使臣以礼,臣事君以忠。" 《论语·八佾》

【今译】孔子回答道:"君主让臣子做事应该以礼待臣;臣子应以忠心报答君主,全心侍奉君主。"

【英译】Confucius answered, "The ruler should employ the service of his subjects in accordance with the rites. A subject should serve his ruler by doing his best."

43. 【原文】子曰:"《关雎》,乐而不淫,哀而不伤。" 《论语·八佾》

【今译】孔子说:"《关雎》这首诗,快乐而不放荡,悲哀而不痛苦。"

【英译】The Master said, "In the *Kuan Chü* there is joy without wantonness, and sorrow without self-injury."

44. 【原文】子闻之,曰:"成事不说,遂事不谏,既往不咎。" 《论语·八佾》

【今译】孔子听说后说:"已经做过的事就不用提了,已经完成的事就不用再去劝阻了,已经过去的事也就不必再追究了。"

【英译】The Master, on hearing of this reply, commented, "One does not explain away what is already done, one does not argue against what is already accomplished, and one does not condemn what has already gone by."

45. 【原文】子曰:"居上不宽,为礼不敬,临丧不哀,吾何以观之哉?"

《论语·八佾》

【今译】孔子说:"居于统治地位而不宽以待人,行礼的时候也不庄严肃穆,对待丧事不真心哀戚,这种样子我怎么能看得下去呢?"

【英译】The Master said, "What can I find worthy of note in a man who is lacking in tolerance when in high position, in reverence when performing the rites and in sorrow when in mourning?"

46. 【原文】子曰:"里仁为美,择不处仁,焉得知?" 《论语·里仁》

【今译】孔子说:"跟仁德的人做邻居才好,如果居住时不选择住在贤德的人的附近,我们又怎么能得到智慧呢?"

【英译】The Master said, "Of neighborhoods benevolence is the most beautiful. How can the man be considered wise who, when he has the choice, does not settle in benevolence?"

47. 【原文】子曰:"不仁者不可以久处约,不可以长处乐。仁者安仁,知者利仁。"

《论语·里仁》

【今译】孔子说:"没有仁德之心的人不能长久地处在贫困中,也不能长久地处于安乐中。有仁德的人安于仁道,有智慧的人则是知道仁对自己有利才去实行仁道的。"

【英译】The Master said, "One who is not benevolent cannot remain long in straitened circumstances, nor can he remain long in easy circumstances. The benevolent man is attracted to benevolence because he feels at home in it. The wise man is attracted to benevolence because he finds it to his advantage."

48. 【原文】子曰:"唯仁者能好人,能恶人。" 《论语·里仁》

【今译】孔子说:"唯有仁德的人能正确地喜欢一个人、厌恶一个人。"

【英译】The Master said, "It is only the benevolent man who is capable of liking or disliking other men."

49. 【原文】子曰:"苟志于仁矣,无恶也。" 《论语·里仁》

【今译】孔子说:"如果立定志向实行仁道的话,总是没有坏处的。"

【英译】The Master said, "If a man sets his heart on benevolence, he will be free from evil."

50. 【原文】子曰:"富与贵,是人之所欲也,不以其道得之,不处也。贫与贱,是人之所恶也,不以其道得之,不去也。" 《论语·里仁》

【今译】孔子说:"财富与地位是每个人所向往的,但不是以正当的方式得到的,君子是不会接受的。贫穷与卑微是每个人所厌恶的,如果不是用正当的手段去改变这种境况,君子宁愿不改变。"

【英译】The Master said, "Wealth and high station are what men desire but unless I got them in the right way, I would not remain in them. Poverty and low station are what men dislike, but if I did not get them in the right way, I would not try to escape from them."

51. 【原文】子曰:"朝闻道,夕死可矣。" 《论语·里仁》

【今译】孔子说:"如果在早上听闻了真理,即使晚上就会死去也没有什么遗憾了。"

【英译】The Master said, "He has not lived in vain who dies the day he is told about the way."

52. 【原文】子曰:"君子怀德,小人怀土;君子怀邢,小人怀惠。" 《论语·里仁》

【今译】孔子说:"君子时刻不忘记德行,小人时刻惦记的只是乡土;君子关心法度,小人关心恩惠。"

【英译】The Master said, "While the gentleman cherishes benign rules, the small man cherishes his native land. While the gentleman cherishes respect for the law, the small man cherishes generous treatment."

53. 【原文】子曰:"君子喻于义,小人喻于利。" 《论语·里仁》

【今译】孔子说:"君子明白的是义,小人只知道利。"

【英译】The Master said, "The gentleman understands what is moral. The small man understands what is profitable."

54. 【原文】子曰:"见贤思齐焉,见不贤而内自省也。" 《论语·里仁》

【今译】孔子说："看见贤德的人就要努力学习向他靠齐，看见不贤德的人就要立即反省自己有没有类似的缺点。"

【英译】The Master said, "When you meet someone better than yourself, turn your thoughts to becoming his equal. When you meet someone not so good as you are, look within and examine your own Self."

55.【原文】子曰："父母在，不远游，游必有方。" 《论语·里仁》

【今译】孔子说："父母在世的时候，不要离开他们去很远的地方，避免他们没有人照顾，不得已而外出必须要告诉他们要去的地方。"

【英译】The Master said, "While your parents are alive, you should not go too far afield in your travels. If you do, your whereabouts should always be known."

56.【原文】子曰："君子欲纳于言而敏于行。" 《论语·里仁》

【今译】孔子说："君子言行要谨慎，行动要勤敏。"

【英译】The Master said, "The gentleman desires to be halting in speech but quick in action."

57.【原文】子曰："德不孤，必有邻。" 《论语·里仁》

【今译】孔子说："有道德的人是不会孤独的，一定会有志同道合的人来与他做伴。"

【英译】The Master said, "Virtue never stands alone. It is bound to have neighbors."

58.【原文】子曰："朽木不可雕也，粪土之墙不可杇也。" 《论语·公冶长》

【今译】孔子说"腐烂了的木头没有办法在上面雕刻，腐土垒起的墙壁没有办法粉刷。"

【英译】The Master said, "A piece of rotten wood cannot be carved, nor can a wall of dried dung be troweled."

59.【原文】子曰："始吾于人也，听其言而信其行；今吾于人也，听其言而观其行。"

《论语·公冶长》

【今译】孔子说："最开始的时候，我观察一个人，听到他所说的话，便相信他的行为；现在我观察一个人，会在听到他的话后，继续考察他的行为。"

【英译】The Master added, "I used to take on trust a man's deeds after having listened to his words. Now having listened to a man's words, I go on to observe his deeds."

60.【原文】子曰："敏而好学，不耻下问。" 《论语·公冶长》

【今译】孔子说："聪明勤勉而又刻苦学习，遇到不懂的问题，随时向人请教，而不在乎别人身份地位的高低。"

【英译】The Master said, "He was quick and eager to learn; he was not ashamed to seek the advice of those who were beneath him in station."

61.【原文】季文子三思而后行。子闻之，曰："再，斯可矣。" 《论语·公冶长》

【今译】季文子每做一件事都要考虑很多次才行动。孔子听说后,说:"想两次就可以了。"

【英译】Chi Wen Tzu always thought many times before taking action. When the Master was told of this, he commented, "Twice is quite enough."

62.【原文】吾闻之也:君子周急不继富。 《论语·雍也》

【今译】我听说过,君子只是雪中送炭,同济急需而不是锦上添花,为富人增富。

【英译】I have heard it said that a gentleman gives to help the needy and not to maintain the rich in style.

63.【原文】子曰:"贤哉,回也!一箪食,一瓢饮,在陋巷,人不堪其忧,回也不改其乐。"
《论语·雍也》

【今译】孔子说:"颜回的品德多么高尚啊!一竹筐篮饭,一瓢水,住在简陋的地方,别人都忍受不了这种穷苦的生活,颜回却没有改变他好学的天性。"

【英译】The Master said, "How admirable Hui is! Living in a mean dwelling on a bowlful of rice and a ladleful of water is a hardship most men would find intolerable, but Hui does not allow this to affect his joy."

64.【原文】子曰:"质胜文则野,文胜质则史。文质彬彬,然后君子。"
《论语·雍也》

【今译】孔子说:"质朴多于文采,就会流于粗俗;文采多于质朴,就会流于虚伪、浮夸。只有质朴和文采配合恰当,才能成为君子。"

【英译】The Master said, "When there is preponderance of native substance over acquired refinement, the result will be churlishness. When there is a preponderance of acquired refinement over native substance, the result will be pedantry. Only a well-balanced admixture of these two will result in gentlemanliness."

65.【原文】子曰:"知之者不如好之者,好之者不如乐之者。" 《论语·雍也》

【今译】孔子说:"对任何学问和事业懂得它的人,不如爱好它的人;爱好它的人,又不如以它为乐的人。"

【英译】The Master said, "To be fond of something is better than merely to know it, and to find joy in it is better than merely to be fond of it."

66.【原文】子曰:"知者乐水,仁者乐山。知者动,仁者静。知者乐,仁者寿。"
《论语·雍也》

【今译】孔子说:"聪明的人爱水,仁德人爱山。聪明人活泼,仁德的人沉静。聪明人快乐,仁德人长寿。"

【英译】The Master said, "The wise find joy in water; the benevolent find joy in mountains. The wise are active; the benevolent are still. The wise are joyful; the benevolent are long-lived."

67. 【原文】子曰:"述而不作,信而好古,窃比于我老彭。"　　　《论语·述而》

    【今译】孔子说:"只传述而不创作,相信并且喜好古代的东西,我私下里把自己比作老彭。"

    【英译】The Master said, "I transmit but not innovate; I am truthful in what I say and devoted to antiquity. I venture to compare myself to our Old Peng."

68. 【原文】子曰:"默而识之,学而不厌,诲人不倦,何有于我哉?"　　　《论语·述而》

    【今译】孔子说:"把所学到的知识默默地记在心里,努力学习而不厌烦,教导别人而不疲倦,这对我有什么困难呢?"

    【英译】The Master said, "Quietly to store up knowledge in my mind, to learn without flagging, to teach without growing weary, these present me with no difficulties."

69. 【原文】子曰:"不义而富且贵,于我如浮云。"　　　《论语·述而》

    【今译】孔子说:"用不正当的手段得来的富与贵,对我来说就像是天空一吹即散的云彩一样。"

    【英译】The Master said, "Wealth and rank attained through immoral means have as much to do with me as passing clouds."

70. 【原文】子曰:"我非生而知之者,好古,敏以求之者也。"　　　《论语·述而》

    【今译】孔子说:"我不是生来就有知识的人,只是爱好古代文化、勤奋敏捷去求索知识的人。"

    【英译】The Master said, "I was not born with knowledge but, being fond of antiquity, I am quick to seek it."

71. 【原文】子曰:"三人行,必有我师焉。择其善者而从之,其不善者而改之。"

    《论语·述而》

    【今译】孔子说:"三个人同行,其中一定有可以为我所取法的人。我选择他善的品德向他学习,看到他不善的地方就作为借鉴,改掉自己的缺点。"

    【英译】The Master said, "Even when walking in the company of two other men, I am bound to be able to learn from them. The good points of the one, I copy; the bad points of the other, I correct in myself."

72. 【原文】子曰:"君子坦荡荡,小人长戚戚。"　　　《论语·述而》

    【今译】孔子说:"君子心胸宽广,小人总是忧愁。"

    【英译】The Master said, "The gentleman is easy of mind, while the small man is always full of anxiety."

73. 【原文】曾子有疾，孟敬子问之。曾子言曰："鸟之将死，其鸣也哀；人之将死，其言也善。"　　　　　　　　　　　　　　　　　　《论语·泰伯》

【今译】曾子有病，孟敬子去探望他。曾子对他说："鸟快死了，它的叫声是悲哀的；人快死了，他说的话是善意的。"

【英译】Tseng Tzu was seriously ill. When Meng Ching Tzu visited him, this was what Tseng Tzu said, "Sad is the cry of a dying bird; good are the words of a dying man."

74. 【原文】曾子曰："士不可以不弘毅，任重而道远。仁以为己任，不亦重乎？死而后已，不亦远乎？"　　　　　　　　　　　　　　　　　　《论语·泰伯》

【今译】曾子说："读书人不可以不刚强而有毅力，因为他责任重大，路程遥远。以实现仁德于天下为自己的责任，难道还不重大吗？奋斗终生，死而后已，难道路程还不遥远吗？"

【英译】Tseng Tzu said, "A gentleman must be strong and resolute, for his burden is heavy and the road is long. He takes benevolence as his burden. Is that not heavy? Only with death does the road come to an end. Is that not long?"

75. 【原文】子曰："不在其位，不谋其政。"　　　　　　《论语·泰伯》

【今译】孔子说："不在那个职位上，就不要去考虑属于那个职位才应该做的事。"

【英译】The Master said, "Do not concern yourself with matters of government unless they are the responsibility of your office."

76. 【原文】子曰："学如不及，犹恐失之。"　　　　　　《论语·泰伯》

【今译】孔子说："做学问就好像在追逐什么东西似的生怕赶不上，赶上了还生怕丢掉了。"

【英译】The Master said, "Even with a man who urges himself on in his studies as though he was losing ground, my fear is still that he may not make it in time."

77. 【原文】子在川上曰："逝者如斯夫！不舍昼夜。"　　《论语·子罕》

【今译】孔子在河边感叹道："消逝的时光就像这河水一样啊，日夜不停地向前流去。"

【英译】While standing by a river, the Master said, "What passes away is, perhaps, like this. Day and night it never lets up."

78. 【原文】子曰："后生可畏，焉知来者之不如今也？"　《论语·子罕》

【今译】孔子说："年轻人是值得敬畏的，怎么就知道后一代不如前一代呢？"

【英译】The Master said, "It is fitting that we should hold the young in awe. How do we know that the generations to come will not be the equal of the present?"

79. 【原文】子曰："三军可夺帅也，匹夫不可夺志也。"　《论语·子罕》

【今译】孔子说："一国军队，可以使它丧失主帅；但一个男子汉，却不能强迫他放弃自己的志向。"

【英译】The Master said, "The three armies can be deprived of their commanding officer, but even a common man cannot be deprived of his purpose."

80.【原文】子曰:"岁寒,然后知松柏之后彫也。" 《论语·子罕》

【今译】孔子说:"只有到了寒冷的季节,才知道松树和柏树是最后凋零的。"

【英译】The Master said, "Only when the cold season comes is the point brought home that the pine and the cypress are the last to lose their leaves."

81.【原文】子曰:"知者不惑,仁者不忧,勇者不惧。" 《论语·子罕》

【今译】孔子说:"聪明的人不会被迷惑,有仁德的人不会忧愁,勇敢的人无所畏惧。"

【英译】The Master said, "The man of wisdom is never in two minds; the man of benevolence never worries; the man of courage is never afraid."

82.【原文】食不语,寝不言。 《论语·乡党》

【今译】吃饭的时候不交谈,睡觉的时候不说话。

【英译】He did not converse at meals, nor did he talk in bed.

83.【原文】席不正,不坐。 《论语·乡党》

【今译】坐席摆放的方法与位置不合礼制,不坐。

【英译】He did not sit, unless his mat was straight.

84.【原文】乡人饮酒,仗者出,斯出矣。 《论语·乡党》

【今译】行乡饮酒礼的仪式结束后,孔子一定要等老年人都出去了,自己才出去。

【英译】When drinking at a village gathering, he left as soon as those carrying walking sticks had left.

《墨子》
Mozi

【简介】《墨子》一书由墨子弟子收集其生平事迹和语录集合而成,成书于战国后期。书中集中体现了他的十个主张,"兼爱""非攻""尚贤""尚同""节用""节葬""非乐""天志""明鬼""非命",在先秦时期影响很大。墨子,名翟,生卒年不详,大致在战国初期(约公元前476年至公元前390年)。他是墨家学派的创始人,是战国时期著名的思想家、教育家、科学家、军事家。

【Introduction】*Mozi* which is about Mozi's life story and sayings was compiled by his disciples in the end of the Warring States period. There are ten propositions in the book: "Universal Love" "Denouncing Aggressive Warfare" "Respecting the Virtuous" "Identifying with the Superior" "Economizing Expenditures" "Simplicity in Funerals" "Against Music" "The Will of Heaven" "On Ghost" "Against Fatalism", which have a great impact in the pre-Qin period. Mozi's given name is Di, and the dates of his birth and death are not clear, but some scholars believe he lived during the early phase of the Warring States period(c.468~376 BC). He is the founder of Mohism, also a famous thinker, educator, scientist and strategist at his time.

1. 【原文】入国而不存其士，则亡国矣。见贤而不急，则缓其君矣。 《墨子·亲士第一》

   【今译】君主执掌国政，如果不亲近、爱惜他的贤士，那就会导致国家灭亡。见到贤士而不立即起用，那他们就会对君主怠慢。

   【英译】If one does not accord preferential treatment to scholars when entrusted with the power to administer the state affairs, he will be ruining the state; if one is not anxious to employ virtuous and talented people upon seeing them, they will be neglecting the monarch.

2. 【原文】非无安居也，我无安心也；非无足财也，我无足心也。 《墨子·亲士第一》

   【今译】并不是没有安适的居所，而是自己没有安定的心；并不是没有足够的钱财，而是自己没有满足的心。

   【英译】It is not that I do not have a comfortable house, but that I feel ill at ease about the homeless; it is not that I do not have sufficient wealth, but that my heart yearns for more to help the poor.

3. 【原文】是故为其所难者，必得其所欲焉，未闻为其所欲，而免其所恶者也。

   《墨子·亲士第一》

   【今译】因此，凡事能从难的做起，就一定能得到自己所想要的东西。没有听说过只做自己喜欢做的事，却能避免自己不喜欢的结果。

   【英译】Hence those who make strict demands on themselves can certainly attain their desires. I have never heard that those who are lenient with them can avoid their dislikes.

4. 【原文】良弓难张，然可以及高入深；良马难乘，然可以任重致远；良才难令，然可以致君见尊。 《墨子·亲士第一》

   【今译】良弓难以拉开，但它可以射到高深处；良马难以驾驭，但它可以负重行远；良才难以指挥，但他们可以辅佐君王，使之处于至尊的地位。

【英译】Good bows are hard to draw, but they can reach greater heights and pierce more deeply. Good horses are hard to ride but they can carry heavier loads and make longer journeys. Talented people are hard to command but they can make the lord all the more respected.

5. 【原文】君子之道也，贫则见廉，富则见义，生则见爱，死则见哀。

《墨子·修身第二》

【今译】君子之道应该是贫困之时表现出廉洁，富贵之时表现出疏财仗义；对于生者表现出慈爱，对于死者表现出哀痛。

【英译】A gentleman should be incorruptible when he is poor and he should be benevolent when he is rich. He should bestow love to the living and express condolences to the dead.

6. 【原文】志不强者智不达，言不信者行不果。 《墨子·修身第二》

【今译】意志不坚强的人是不会变得聪明的，说话不讲信用的人行动是不会果敢的。

【英译】He who does not have a strong will can hardly have high intelligence; he who does not keep his promise can hardly act resolutely.

7. 【原文】天下从事者不可以无法仪，无法仪而其事能成者无也。 《墨子·法仪第四》

【今译】天下无论从事什么工作的人，都不可以没有法度，没有法度而能把事情办成功的是没有的。

【英译】No matter what kind of business one is engaged in, one must have standards. No one can do his job well without sticking to standards.

8. 【原文】爱人利人者，天必福之；恶人贼人者，天必祸之。 《墨子·法仪第四》

【今译】爱人、利人的，天一定会赐福于他；厌恶人、残害人的，天一定会降祸于他。

【英译】Heaven will bless those who love and help each other and curse those who hate and harm each other.

9. 【原文】仓无备粟，不可以待凶饥。库无备兵，虽有义不能征无义。《墨子·七患第五》

【今译】仓库里没有储备粮食，就不能抵御凶饥之灾。府库里没有储备兵器，即使自己是正义的也不能征讨不义的。

【英译】If there are not enough grains stored in the granaries, we can hardly resist famine or the general scarcity of food. If there is not sufficient weaponry stored in the arsenals, we can hardly have the power to punish the unjust even though we are justified in doing so.

10. 【原文】俭节则昌，淫佚则亡。 《墨子·辞过第六》

【今译】节俭就昌盛，淫逸就灭亡。

【英译】Temperance and economy can lead to prosperity while indulgence and excess only result in destruction.

11. 【原文】尚贤之为政本也。　　　　　　　　　　　　　　　《墨子·尚贤中第九》

　　【今译】尚贤是为政的根本。

　　【英译】Respecting the virtuous and talented is the fundamental policy to govern a country.

12. 【原文】故古圣王以审以尚贤使能为政，而取法于天。　　《墨子·尚贤中第九》

　　【今译】所以古代圣王能审慎地以尚贤使能为政，而取法于天。

　　【英译】The ancient sage kings followed the ways of heaven in honoring the virtuous and employing the talented in government.

13. 【原文】有力者疾以助人，有财者勉以分人，有道者劝以教人。《墨子·尚贤下第十》

　　【今译】有力气的人赶快用力帮助人，有财富的人努力分给别人，有高尚品德的人则要尽力教诲别人。

　　【英译】Those who have strength should lose no time in helping others; those who have wealth should endeavor to share it with others; those who are well versed in Tao should try their best to teach others.

14. 【原文】尚贤者，天鬼百姓之利，而政事之本也。　　　　《墨子·尚贤下第十》

　　【今译】所谓尚贤，是天鬼百姓的利益，是政事的根本啊！

　　【英译】They must take into consideration the principle of respecting the virtuous and talented, for it conforms to the interests of heaven, ghosts and spirits and the people as well as the fundamental policy to govern a country.

15. 【原文】天下兼相爱则治，交相恶则乱。　　　　　　　　《墨子·兼爱上第十四》

　　【今译】天下人全都相亲、相爱则治，相互仇恨则乱。

　　【英译】Universal love will bring peace and order to the world while mutual hatred can only throw the world into disorder.

16. 【原文】仁人之事者，必务求兴天下之利，除天下之害。　《墨子·兼爱下第十六》

　　【今译】仁人的政事，一定要努力兴天下的利，除天下的害。

　　【英译】The benevolent always take it as their duty to promote what is beneficial and eliminate what is disastrous to the people in the world.

17. 【原文】投我以桃，报之以李。　　　　　　　　　　　　《墨子·兼爱下第十六》

　　【今译】别人赠给我红桃，我即报答人家以好李。

　　【英译】Throw me a peach, and I'll return you a plum.

18. 【原文】仁者之为天下度也，辟之无以异乎孝子之为亲度也。

　　　　　　　　　　　　　　　　　　　　　　　　　　《墨子·节葬下第二十五》

　　【今译】仁者们为天下打算，与孝子为父母打算没有什么两样。

　　【英译】There is little difference between the benevolent working for the interests of the people and a filial son working for the interests of his parents.

19. 【原文】我为天之所欲，天亦为我所欲。　　　　《墨子·天志上第二十六》

【今译】我做了天所希望的事，天也会赐给我所要求的东西。

【英译】As we are doing what heaven favors, heaven will do what we favor.

20. 【原文】天下有义则治，无义则乱。　　　　《墨子·天志下第二十八》

【今译】天下有义就安定，无义就祸乱。

【英译】If there is righteousness, the world is in order; if there is not righteousness, the world will fall into disorder.

21. 【原文】然而正者，无自下正上者，必自上正下。　　　　《墨子·天志下第二十八》

【今译】然而讲到正，不是由下边来匡正上边，必定从上边去匡正下边。

【英译】The inferiors cannot decide what is right for the superiors. Only the superiors can decide what is right for the inferiors.

22. 【原文】利人乎，即为；不利人乎，即止。　　　　《墨子·非乐上第三十二》

【今译】有利于人的事就去做，不利于人的事就不做。

【英译】They will do whatever is beneficial to the people and reject whatever is harmful to them.

23. 【原文】义人在上，天下必治，上帝山川鬼神，必有干主，万民被其大利。

《墨子·非命上第三十五》

【今译】有义之人在上位，天下一定大治，上帝、山川和鬼神，必定有宗主祭祀，万民将得到大利。

【英译】When righteous men are in authority, the world will have order, the God, the hills and rivers and ghosts and spirits will have worshipers to offer sacrifice to them, and the people will be greatly benefited.

24. 【原文】入则孝慈于亲戚，出则弟长于乡里，坐处有度，出入有节，男女有辨。

《墨子·非命上第三十五》

【今译】人们在家能孝顺父母，出外能敬爱乡亲，举止有规矩，进出有礼节，男女有分别。

【英译】The virtuous people were filial to their parents at home and respectful to their elders in the village. They were temperate in their conduct, moderate in going out and coming in and decent in their relation with the opposite sex.

25. 【原文】今天下之士君子，忠实欲天下之富而恶其贫，欲天下之治而恶其乱，执有命者之言，不可不非，此天下之大害也。　　　　《墨子·非命上第三十五》

【今译】当今天下的士君子，心中真想求得天下富足而厌恶天下贫穷，想求得天下太平而厌恶天下动乱，那么对于主张有命的人所说的话，就不能不加以反对，因为这些言论是天下的大祸害。

【英译】If the elite gentlemen of today really wish to enrich the world and abolish poverty, and really wish to bring order to the world and hate to see it fall into chaos again, they must condemn the fatalist view, for it is indeed very harmful.

26.【原文】有本之者，有原之者，有用之者。　　　　《墨子·非命中第三十六》

【今译】对事要追根溯源，要推究事情的缘由，要应用于实践。

【英译】They are the standard of investigating historical facts, the standard of verifying the true facts and the standard of application and observation.

27.【原文】有闻之，有见之，谓之有；莫之闻，莫之见，谓之亡。

《墨子·非命中第三十六》

【今译】有人说过、见过就说有，没有听过、见过就说无。

【英译】If there is testimony to prove that someone heard it or saw it, I will say there is fate. If there is no testimony to prove that someone heard it or saw it, I will say there is no fate.

28.【原文】必使饥者得食，寒者得衣，劳者得息，乱者得治。《墨子·非命下第三十七》

【今译】一定要使饥者得食，寒者得衣，劳者得息，乱者得治。

【英译】We must feed the hungry, clothe the cold, allow the weary to rest and restore order in the world.

29.【原文】彼以为强必治，不强必乱，强必宁，不强必危，故不敢怠倦。

《墨子·非命下第三十七》

【今译】他们认为勤必治，不勤必乱，勤必宁，不勤必危，所以不敢懈怠。

【英译】It is because they realize that diligence will bring about order while negligence will result in chaos, and that diligence will produce safety while negligence will lead to danger.

30.【原文】今天下之士君子，中实将欲求兴天下之利，除天下之害，当若有命者之言，不可不强非也。　　　　　　　　　　　　　　　《墨子·非命下第三十七》

【今译】当今天下的士君子，心中真想求兴天下之利，除天下之害，对主张有命的说法，不能不极力加以反对。

【英译】If the elite gentlemen of today really want to promote what is beneficial and abolish what is harmful, they must oppose the assertions of the fatalists.

31.【原文】亲亲有术，尊贤有等。　　　　　　　　　《墨子·非儒下第三十九》

【今译】爱亲人当因亲人有等差而有区别，尊重贤者当因贤者有差异而有不同。

【英译】There are differences to be observed in showing love to one's relatives and there are distinctions to be made in showing respect for the virtuous.

32.【原文】仁，体爱也。　　　　　　　　　　　　　　　　《墨子·经上第四十》

【今译】仁慈，就是对任何一个部分都亲近爱护。

【英译】Benevolence is love in individual cases.

33.【原文】义，利也。　　　　　　　　　　　　　　　　　《墨子·经上第四十》

【今译】义气，就是有利于人。

【英译】Righteousness is the benefit brought to the people.

34.【原文】孝，利亲也。　　　　　　　　　　　　　　　　《墨子·经上第四十》

【今译】孝敬，就是爱利双亲。

【英译】Filial piety is one's devotion to his parents.

35.【原文】卧，知无知也。　　　　　　　　　　　　　　　《墨子·经上第四十》

【今译】睡觉，是感知官能处在无知觉的状态。

【英译】Sleep is a state in which one's perceptual ability is not functioning.

36.【原文】为，穷知而俱于欲也。　　　　　　　　　　　　《墨子·经上第四十》

【今译】错误的行为，是知识短缺、被欲望所支配而造成的。

【英译】The conduct of a man will follow the bent of his desire if he is at his wits' end.

37.【原文】功，利民也。　　　　　　　　　　　　　　　　《墨子·经上第四十》

【今译】功绩，是有利于人民的。

【英译】Meritorious deeds are beneficial to the people.

38.【原文】不知其数而知其尽也，说在明者。　　　　　　《墨子·经下第四十一》

【今译】不知道天下的人数而知其尽爱，是因为有询问了解的缘故。

【英译】We love all the people in the universe without knowing their number, for we are clear about the number of people we may ask.

39.【原文】取下以求上也，说在泽。　　　　　　　　　　《墨子·经下第四十一》

【今译】取得下面的信任才能求得上位，如同水泽善处下位。

【英译】One may choose to stay below for the sake of going up; for example, the water of a pond that stays below will rise at the appropriate time.

40.【原文】有之不必然，无之必不然。　　　　　　　　《墨子·经说上第四十二》

【今译】有了它，不一定能成此现象；没有它，一定不能成此现象。

【英译】It is not certain that the minor cause will bring about the present state of things, but it is certain that the absence of the minor cause will not bring about the present state of things.

41. 【原文】久，古今旦暮。宇，东西家南北。 　　　　　《墨子·经说上第四十二》

【今译】宙包含古、今、旦、暮等一切不同的时间。宇包含东、西、家、南、北等一切不同的空间。

【英译】Time is composed of the ancient and the present, the morning and the evening. Space is composed of north, south, east, west, and your home in the middle.

42. 【原文】举之则轻，废之则重，非有力也。 　　　　　《墨子·经说下第四十三》

【今译】举起羽毛则很轻，放下石头则很重，不必怀疑力的大小。

【英译】If someone lifts something light such as a feather or puts down something heavy such as a rock, he might not be taken as a strong man.

43. 【原文】智少而不学，必寡。 　　　　　《墨子·经说下第四十三》

【今译】知识少而不学，功绩一定很小。

【英译】If you have little knowledge but do not want to learn, you can achieve very little.

44. 【原文】智而不教，功适息。 　　　　　《墨子·经说下第四十三》

【今译】虽有知识而不教人，功绩也只会灭绝了。

【英译】If you have much knowledge but do not want to teach, your knowledge will come to naught.

45. 【原文】仁，爱也。义，利也。 　　　　　《墨子·经说下第四十三》

【今译】仁是爱，义是利。

【英译】To be benevolent is to love others and to be righteous is to benefit others.

46. 【原文】义，利。不义，害。 　　　　　《墨子·大取第四十四》

【今译】讲义，就会有利于人。不讲义，就会有害于人。

【英译】Righteousness is the benefit while unrighteousness is the harm.

47. 【原文】诸圣人所先为，人欲名实。名实不必名。 　　　　　《墨子·大取第四十四》

【今译】圣人们首先要做的是考核声名与实际，人要名实相符。然而有名不一定有实，有实不一定有名。

【英译】The first thing that a sage does is to straighten out the relationship between name and entity. The name does not necessarily match the entity and the entity is not necessarily the same as the name.

48. 【原文】爱人之亲若爱其亲，其类在官苟。兼爱相若，一爱相若。

《墨子·大取第四十四》

【今译】爱别人的父母如同爱自己的父母。同等地敬爱别人的父母，那么，自己的父母自然也在别人的敬爱之中。兼爱相同，爱一人与爱众人相同。

【英译】We should love others' parents in the same way as we love our own parents. We should love everybody in the same way.

49. 【原文】夫辩者,将以明是非之分,审治乱之纪,明同异之处,察名实之理,处利害,决嫌疑。 　　　　《墨子·小取第四十五》

【今译】论辩的目的是要区别是非,审查治乱的规律,分清同与不同之所在,考察名称和实际的原理,处理利害,决断嫌疑。

【英译】The purpose of disputation is to distinguish clearly between right and wrong, inquire into the principles of order and misrule, clarify the points of sameness and difference, discern the patterns of names and objects, judge the benefits and harms, and resolve confusions and doubts.

50. 【原文】可誉而不誉,非仁也。 　　　　《墨子·耕柱第四十六》

【今译】应该赞美别人却不加以赞美,那就不仁了。

【英译】Not to praise what should be praised is not benevolent.

51. 【原文】言足以复行者,常之;不足以举行者,勿常。不足以举行而常之,是荡口也。
　　　　《墨子·耕柱第四十六》

【今译】说话能付之于行动,就不妨常说,不能够实行的就不要常说。不能够实行而又常说,这就是徒费口舌。

【英译】Words that can be put into action should be spoken frequently; words that cannot be put into action should not be spoken too often. To speak frequently about what cannot be put into action is the same as to speak nonsense.

52. 【原文】凡言凡动,利于天鬼百姓者为之;凡言凡动,害于天鬼百姓者舍之。
　　　　《墨子·贵义第四十七》

【今译】凡言语、行动有利于天神百姓的就去做,凡言语、行动有害于天神百姓的要舍弃。

【英译】Any word or action that is beneficial to heaven, to ghosts and spirits and to the people is to be accepted; any word or action that is harmful to heaven, to ghosts and spirits and to the people is to be abandoned.

53. 【原文】嘿则思,言则诲,动则事。 　　　　《墨子·贵义第四十七》

【今译】沉默时可以深思,出言时能给人教诲,行动时能办成事。

【英译】When we are silent, we should be in deep thoughts; when we speak, we should be able to teach; when we take actions, we should be able to make achievements.

54. 【原文】以其言非吾言者,是犹以卵投石也。 　　　　《墨子·贵义第四十七》

【今译】拿他的言论来反对我的言论,这好比拿鸡蛋来击石头。

【英译】Refuting my words with those of others is the same as throwing eggs against a stone.

55. 【原文】君子共己以待，问焉则言，不问焉则止。譬若钟然，扣则鸣，不扣则不鸣。

《墨子·公孟第四十八》

【今译】君子要拱手以待，问则说，不问则不说，像钟一样，敲则响，不敲则不响。

【英译】A gentleman should fold his hands and wait. And he should speak when being asked and keep quiet when not being asked. A gentleman is like a bell which will sound when being struck and will remain silent when not being struck.

56. 【原文】有义不义，无祥不祥。　　　　　　　　　　　　《墨子·公孟第四十八》

【今译】人有义与不义之分，但不因为义而得福，不因为不义而得祸。

【英译】Righteousness and unrighteousness do exist, but fortune and disaster are not brought about by righteousness or unrighteousness.

57. 【原文】夫义，天下之大器也，何以视人必强为之？　　《墨子·公孟第四十八》

【今译】义，是天下最可贵的东西，为什么一定要看他人行事呢？

【英译】Righteousness is the greatest thing in the world. Why should one follow others in pursuing it？

58. 【原文】施人薄而望人厚，则人唯恐其有赐于己也。　　《墨子·鲁问第四十九》

【今译】如果施给人家的很薄而希望人家报答丰厚，那么人家就害怕你再施给他了。

【英译】If you give very little to others and expect too much from them, they will feel uneasy when you give them more gifts.

59. 【原文】故交相爱，交相恭，犹若相利也。　　　　　　《墨子·鲁问第四十九》

【今译】所以要交相爱，交相恭，这样才能相利。

【英译】Therefore, mutual love and mutual respect can bring mutual benefit.

60. 【原文】交相钩，交相强，犹若相害也。　　　　　　　《墨子·鲁问第四十九》

【今译】交相钩，交相镶，这就会相互损害。

【英译】The mutual pulling and pursuing are just mutual injury.

61. 【原文】安国之道，道任地始，地得其任则功成，地不得其任则劳而无功。

《墨子·号令第七十》

【今译】安定国家的方法，先从道适应地利开始。适应地利则成功，不适应地利则劳而无功。

【英译】The way to secure a state starts with the use of its favorable geographical conditions. Effective use of the country's geographical conditions can lead to success while the ineffective use of the country's geographical conditions can result in waste of labor.

62. 【原文】使人各得其所长，天下事当，钧其分职，天下事得，皆其所喜，天下事备，

强弱有数，天下事具矣。　　　　　　　　　　　　　　　《墨子·杂守第七十一》

【今译】用人能发挥其长处，才算用人得当；分配均衡，各司其职，事情才能办好；各人都得到了喜爱的东西，强与弱心中有定数，这样治理天下才算成功。

【英译】If everyone's talent can be brought into full play, everything in the world can be dealt with properly; if everyone's job responsibility is properly shared, everything in the world can be accomplished; if everyone is allowed to do what he likes, he will get everything ready; if everyone knows his weak points as well as his strong points, everything can be done perfectly.

《孟子》
Mencius

【简介】《孟子》是记录孟子言行的一部著作，是由孟子及其弟子在战国中期所著，是"四书"之一，是儒家经典中的一个重要组成部分，进一步发展了孔子的思想。孟子（约公元前372年至公元前289年），名轲，字子舆，是战国中期鲁国人，著名的思想家、政治家、教育家，孔子学说的继承者，儒家重要代表人物。

【Introduction】*Mencius* which records the words and deeds of Mencius was written in the middle of the Warring States period by Mencius and his disciples. As one of The Four Books and the important component of the classics of the Confucian school, it further develops Confucian ideology. Mencius(c.372~289 BC) named Ke, alias Ziyu, is a native of Lu of the Warring States period. He is a great thinker, statesman and educator, also a significant successor and representative of Confucian doctrine.

1. 【原文】古之人与民偕乐，故能乐也。　　　　　　　　　《孟子·梁惠王章句上》

   【今译】就因为他愿和老百姓同享欢乐，所以他能够得到真正的快乐。

   【英译】As the ancient king enjoyed these things together with the people, he was able to enjoy them.

2. 【原文】以五十步笑百步，则何如？　　　　　　　　　　《孟子·梁惠王章句上》

   【今译】那些跑了五十步的士兵，竟耻笑跑一百步的士兵，说他胆子太小，行不行呢？

【英译】Do you think those who have run fifty paces are entitled to laugh at those who have run a hundred paces?

3. 【原文】庖有肥肉，厩有肥马，民有饥色，野有饿莩，此率兽而食人也。

《孟子·梁惠王章句上》

【今译】您的厨房里有皮薄膘肥的肉，您的马厩里有健壮的马，可是老百姓面带饥色，野外躺着饿死的尸体，这简直是在上位的人率领着禽兽来吃人。

【英译】In your kitchen there is fat meat; in your stables there are strong horses. But your people look starved, and in the countryside there are people dead from famine. That amounts to leading beasts out to devour men.

4. 【原文】仲尼曰："始作俑者，其无后乎！"

《孟子·梁惠王章句上》

【今译】孔子说过："第一个造作木偶、土偶来殉葬的，该会绝子灭孙、断绝后代吧！"

【英译】Confucius said, "He who first made wooden or clay figures to bury with the dead must have had no posterity."

5. 【原文】仁者无敌。

《孟子·梁惠王章句上》

【今译】仁德的人是无敌于天下的。

【英译】A benevolent ruler never meets his match.

6. 【原文】是以君子远庖厨也。

《孟子·梁惠王章句上》

【今译】所以，君子把厨房设在远离自己的地方，就是这个道理。

【英译】That is why a gentleman keeps away from his kitchen.

7. 【原文】夫子言之，于我心有戚戚焉。

《孟子·梁惠王章句上》

【今译】您老人家这么一说，我的心便豁然明亮了。

【英译】What you say has touched my heart.

8. 【原文】吾力足以举百钧，而不足以举一羽；明足以察秋毫之末，而不见舆薪。

《孟子·梁惠王章句上》

【今译】我的气力能够举起三千斤重，却拿不起一根羽毛；我的目力能够把秋天鸟的羽绒看得分明，而一车子的柴火摆在眼前却瞧不见。

【英译】I am strong enough to lift three thousand catties, but I cannot lift one feather; I can see clearly the tip of a tiny hair, but I cannot see a cartload of fagots.

9. 【原文】老吾老，以及人之老；幼吾幼，以及人之幼。

《孟子·梁惠王章句上》

【今译】尊敬自己的长辈，从而推广到尊敬别人的长辈；爱护自己的儿女，从而推广到爱护别人的儿女。

【英译】Do reverence to the elders in your own family and extend it to those in other families; show loving care to the young in your own family and extend it to those in other families.

10. 【原文】故推恩足以保四海，不推恩无以保妻子。 《孟子·梁惠王章句上》

【今译】所以，由近及远把恩惠推广开去，便足以安定天下；不这样，甚至连自己的妻子和孩子都保不了。

【英译】Therefore, if one extends one's kindness, one will be able to protect the whole world; if not, one will not be able to protect one's wife and children.

11. 【原文】权，然后知轻重；度，然后知长短。 《孟子·梁惠王章句上》

【今译】称一称，才晓得轻重；量一量，才晓得长短。

【英译】Only by weighing a thing, can you know its weight; and only by measuring it, can you know its length.

12. 【原文】缘木求鱼，虽不得鱼，无后灾。 《孟子·梁惠王章句上》

【今译】爬上树去捉鱼，虽然捉不到，却没有祸害。

【英译】If you try to find fish by climbing a tree, though in vain, there will be no disaster.

13. 【原文】然则小固不可以敌大，寡固不可以敌众，弱固不可以敌强。

《孟子·梁惠王章句上》

【今译】从这里便可以看出：小国不可以跟大国为敌，人口稀少的国家不可以跟人口众多的国家为敌，弱国不可以跟强国为敌。

【英译】This serves to show that the small can not cope with the big, the few can not cope with the many, and the weak can not cope with the strong.

14. 【原文】谨庠序之教，申之以孝悌之义，颁白者不负戴于道路矣。

《孟子·梁惠王章句上》

【今译】办好各类学校，反复地用孝顺父母、尊敬兄长的大道理来开导他们，那么，须发花白的人便会有人代劳不致头顶着、背负着物件在路上行走了。

【英译】Let careful attention be paid to education in local schools, where the significance of filial and fraternal duties is stressed repeatedly, and grey-haired people will not be carrying loads on the roads.

15. 【原文】曰："独乐乐，与人乐乐，孰乐？"曰："不若与人。"曰："与少乐乐，与众乐乐，孰乐？"曰："不若与众。" 《孟子·梁惠王章句下》

【今译】孟子说："一个人单独地欣赏音乐快乐，跟别人一起欣赏音乐也快乐，究竟哪一种更快乐些呢？"

齐王说："当然跟别人一起欣赏音乐更快乐些。"

孟子说："跟少数人欣赏音乐快乐，跟多数人欣赏音乐也快乐，究竟哪一种更快乐些呢？"

齐王说："当然跟多数人一起欣赏音乐更快乐些。"

【英译】"Which is the more delightful, enjoyment by yourself or enjoyment along with others?"

"Along with others."

"Which is the more delightful, enjoyment along with a few or enjoyment along with many?"

"Along with many."

16. 【原文】今王与百姓同乐，则王矣。　　　　　　　　　　《孟子·梁惠王章句下》

    【今译】如果王同百姓同享快乐，就可以使天下归服了。

    【英译】"Now, if you share your enjoyment with the people, you will be able to unify the whole world."

17. 【原文】乐天者保天下，畏天者保其国。　　　　　　　　《孟子·梁惠王章句下》

    【今译】无往而不快乐的人足以安定天下，谨慎畏惧的人足以保护住自己的国家。

    【英译】He who delights in heaven's mandate will be able to stabilize the world, while he who stands in awe of heaven's mandate will be able to stabilize his own state.

18. 【原文】乐民之乐者，民亦乐其乐；忧民之忧者，民亦忧其忧。

    《孟子·梁惠王章句下》

    【今译】以百姓的快乐为自己的快乐，百姓也会以国王的快乐为自己的快乐；以百姓的忧愁为自己的忧愁，百姓也会以国王的忧愁为自己的忧愁。

    【英译】The people will delight in the joy of a ruler who delights in their joy, and will grieve at the sorrow of a ruler who grieves at their sorrow.

19. 【原文】老而无妻曰鳏，老而无夫曰寡，老而无子曰独，幼而无父曰孤。

    《孟子·梁惠王章句下》

    【今译】失掉妻室的老年人叫作鳏夫，失掉丈夫的老妇人叫作寡妇，没有儿女的老人叫作孤独者，死了父亲的儿童叫作孤儿。

    【英译】Old men without wives, old women without husbands, old people without children, young people without fathers—these four kinds of common people are most miserable as they have no one to help them.

20. 【原文】见其礼而知其政，闻其乐而知其德。　　　　　　《孟子·公孙丑章句上》

    【今译】看到一国的礼制，就了解它的政治；听到一国的音乐，就知道它的德教。

    【英译】From the rites of a state he could see its government and from its music he could see the private morality of the ruler.

21. 【原文】圣人之于民，亦类也。出于其类，拔乎其萃。

    《孟子·公孙丑章句上》

    【今译】圣人对于百姓，也是同类，但远远超出了他那同类，大大高出了他那一群。

【英译】The sage is also a kind of man. But he stands out of the common run and preeminently excels other men.

22. 【原文】天作孽，犹可违；自作孽，不可活。　　　　　　　　《孟子·公孙丑章句上》

   【今译】天降的灾害，还可以躲避；自己造的罪孽，逃也逃不了。

   【英译】When trouble befalls you from heaven, there is still hope of avoidance; when you ask for trouble, there is no hope of escape.

23. 【原文】恻隐之心，仁之端也；羞恶之心，义之端也；辞让之心，礼之端也；是非之心，智之端也。　　　　　　　　　　　　　　　　　　　　　　　　　　　　《孟子·公孙丑章句上》

   【今译】同情之心是仁的开端，羞耻之心是义的开端，推让之心是礼的开端，是非之心是智的开端。

   【英译】The sense of compassion is the beginning of benevolence; the sense of shame is the beginning of righteousness; the sense of modesty is the beginning of decorum; the sense of right and wrong is the beginning of wisdom.

24. 【原文】天时不如地利，地利不如人和。　　　　　　　　　《孟子·公孙丑章句下》

   【今译】有利的时机和气候条件不如有利的地势，有利的地势不如人的齐心协力。

   （李晓婧译）

   【英译】For defence in warfare the favorable weather is not so important as the topographical advantage, and the topographical advantage is not so important as the group morale.

25. 【原文】得道者多助，失道者寡助。　　　　　　　　　　　《孟子·公孙丑章句下》

   【今译】行仁政，帮助他的人就多；不行仁政，帮助他的人就少。

   【英译】One who has the moral force will have many to support him, and one who has not the moral force will have few to support him.

26. 【原文】上有好者，下必有甚焉者矣。　　　　　　　　　　《孟子·滕文公章句上》

   【今译】在上位的有什么爱好，在下面的人一定爱好得更厉害。

   【英译】If people of high rank are fond of something, people in inferior position will like it better.

   （李晓婧改译）

27. 【原文】君子之德，风也；小人之德，草也。　　　　　　　《孟子·滕文公章句上》

   【今译】君子的行为好像风，小人的行为好像草，风向哪边吹，草就向哪边倒。

   【英译】The virtue of people above is like wind, while the virtue of people below is like grass. The grass is sure to bend if swept over by the wind.

28. 【原文】民之为道也，有恒产者有恒心，无恒产者无恒心。　《孟子·滕文公章句上》

   【今译】有一定的财产收入的人，才有一定的道德观念和行为准则；没有一定的财产收入的人，便不会有一定的道德观念和行为准则。

【英译】Those who have constant means of livelihood will have constant hearts, and those who have no constant means of livelihood will not have constant hearts.

29. 【原文】为富不仁矣，为仁不富矣。 《孟子·滕文公章句上》

【今译】要发财致富，便不能仁爱了；要仁爱，便不能发财致富了。

【英译】Those who seek to be rich cannot be benevolent; those who seek to be benevolent cannot be rich.

30. 【原文】劳心者治人，劳力者治于人。 《孟子·滕文公章句上》

【今译】干脑力劳动的人统治人，干体力劳动的人被人统治。

【英译】Those who work with their minds rule others; those who work with their strength are ruled by others.

31. 【原文】父子有亲，君臣有义，夫妇有别，长幼有叙，朋友有信。

《孟子·滕文公章句上》

【今译】父子之间有骨肉之亲，君臣之间有礼仪之道，夫妻之间挚爱而有内外之别，老少之间有尊卑之序，朋友之间有诚信之德。

【英译】The people might be taught the human relationships, namely, affection between father and son, righteousness between ruler and subject, distinction between husband and wife, orderly sequence between old and young, and fidelity between friends.

32. 【原文】富贵不能淫，贫贱不能移，威武不能屈，此之谓大丈夫。

《孟子·滕文公章句下》

【今译】富裕尊贵不能乱我之心，贫穷卑贱不能变我之志，权势武力不能屈我之节，这样才叫作大丈夫。

【英译】He cannot be led into dissipation by wealth and rank, nor deflected from his aim by poverty and obscurity, nor made to bend by power and force—all these are characteristics of a great man.

33. 【原文】父母之心，人皆有之。不待父母之命、媒妁之言，钻穴隙相窥，逾墙相从，则父母国人皆贱之。 《孟子·滕文公章句下》

【今译】爹娘这种心情，个个都有。但是，若不等爹娘开口，不经媒人介绍，自己便钻洞扒门缝来互相偷看，爬过墙去私自会面，那么，爹娘和社会人士都会看不起他。

【英译】Such a parental wish is common to all human beings. But those young people will be despised by parents and fellow-countrymen alike, if they bore holes in the wall to peep at each other, and climb over the wall to be with each other without waiting for the orders of the parents and the arrangement of a matchmaker.

34. 【原文】入则孝，出则悌，守先王之道，以待后之学者。 《孟子·滕文公章句下》

【今译】在家孝顺父母，出外尊敬长辈，严守古代圣王的礼法道义，并用来扶植后代学者。

【英译】Here there is a man who, filial to his parents and respectful to his elders, adheres to the principles of the ancient saintly kings and whom the younger generation can learn from.

35.【原文】民之望之，若大旱之望雨也。 《孟子·滕文公章句下》

【今译】老百姓盼望他，正和大旱年岁盼望雨水一样。

【英译】The people longed for his arrival as they longed for rain in a long spell of drought.

36.【原文】救民于水火之中，取其残而已矣。 《孟子·滕文公章句下》

【今译】把老百姓从水火之中拯救出来，杀掉残暴的君主罢了。

【英译】The king of Zhou saved the people from fire and water only by killing their tyrannical rulers.

37.【原文】离娄之明、公输子之巧，不以规矩，不能成方圆。 《孟子·离娄章句上》

【今译】就是有古时明者离娄的眼力、巧匠公输般的技巧，如果不用圆规和曲尺，也不能正确地画出方形和圆形。

【英译】Even with the sharp eyes of Li Lou and the skill of Gongshuzi, one would not be able to form squares and circles without a carpenter's square and compass.

38.【原文】天下之本在国，国之本在家，家之本在身。 《孟子·离娄章句上》

【今译】天下的根本是国，国的根本是家，而家的根本则是个人。

【英译】This shows that the world is based on the state, the state on the family, and the family on the individual.

39.【原文】顺天者存，逆天者亡。 《孟子·离娄章句上》

【今译】顺应大势的生存，违背大势的灭亡。

【英译】Those who submit to heaven live; those who go against heaven perish.

40.【原文】夫人必自侮，然后人侮之；家必自毁，而后人毁之；国必自伐，而后人伐之。

《孟子·离娄章句上》

【今译】所以一个人一定先有自取侮辱的行为，别人才会侮辱他；一个家庭一定先有自取毁灭的因素，别人才毁灭它；一个国家一定先有自取讨伐的原因，别人才讨伐它。

【英译】A man is insulted only when he has insulted himself. A family is destroyed only when it has destroyed itself. A state is attacked only when it has attacked itself.

41.【原文】恭者不侮人，俭者不夺人。 《孟子·离娄章句上》

【今译】恭敬别人的人不会侮辱别人，自己节俭的人不会掠夺别人。

【英译】A respectable man does not insult others; a frugal man does not rob others.

42. 【原文】人之患在好为人师。　　　　　　　　　　　　　　《孟子·离娄章句上》

【今译】一个人的毛病，就在于喜欢在别人面前称老师。

【英译】The trouble with people is their being too ready to teach others.

43. 【原文】不孝有三，无后为大。　　　　　　　　　　　　　《孟子·离娄章句上》

【今译】不孝顺父母的事有三件，其中以没有子孙后代为最重大。

【英译】There are three things that are considered as unfilial, and the worst of them is to have no posterity.

44. 【原文】仁者爱人，有礼者敬人。　　　　　　　　　　　　《孟子·离娄章句下》

【今译】仁德的人爱别人，有礼貌的人尊敬别人。

【英译】A man of benevolence loves others; a man of decorum respects others.

45. 【原文】爱人者，人恒爱之；敬人者，人恒敬之。　　　　　《孟子·离娄章句下》

【今译】爱别人的人，别人经常爱他；尊敬别人的人，别人经常尊敬他。

【英译】One who loves others is always loved by others; one who respects others is always respected by others.

46. 【原文】父母爱之，喜而不忘；父母恶之，劳而不怨。　　　《孟子·万章章句上》

【今译】父母喜爱他，虽然高兴，却不因此懈怠；父母厌恶他，虽然惆怅，却不因此怨恨。

【英译】When a man's parents love him, he is happy, but he is not supposed to be negligent; when his parents dislike him, he is naturally unhappy, but he is not supposed to be aggrieved.

47. 【原文】伯夷，目不视恶色，耳不听恶声。　　　　　　　　《孟子·万章章句下》

【今译】伯夷，眼睛不去看不好的事物，耳朵不去听不好的声音。

【英译】Boyi turned a blind eye to offensive sights and a deaf ear to offensive sounds.

48. 【原文】天之生斯民也，使先知觉后知，使先觉觉后觉。　　《孟子·万章章句下》

【今译】上天生育这些百姓，就是要先知先觉的人来开导后知后觉的人。

【英译】Heaven, in creating the world's people, makes men who have foresight awaken those who have not, and it makes men who have been awakened awaken those who have not.

49. 【原文】食色，性也。仁，内也，非外也；义，外也，非内也。《孟子·告子章句上》

【今译】饮食男女，这是人的本性。仁是发自内心的东西，不是从外面来的；义是外来的东西，不是发自内心的。

【英译】Eating and sex are human nature. Benevolence is internal, not external while righteousness is external, not internal.

50. 【原文】恻隐之心，人皆有之；羞恶之心，人皆有之；恭敬之心，人皆有之；是非之心，人皆有之。

　　　　　　　　　　　　　　　　　　　　　　　　　　　《孟子·告子章句上》

【今译】同情之心，每个人都有；羞耻之心，每个人都有；恭敬之心，每个人都有；是非之心，每个人都有。

【英译】Compassion is a feeling shared by everyone, so is shame, so is respect, so is the sense of right and wrong.

51.【原文】鱼，我所欲也，熊掌亦我所欲也；二者不可得兼，舍鱼而取熊掌者也。生亦我所欲也，义亦我所欲也；二者不可得兼，舍生而取义者也。　　《孟子·告子章句上》

【今译】鱼是我所喜欢的，熊掌也是我所喜欢的；如果两者不能都拥有，便放弃鱼，而要熊掌。生命是我所喜欢的，道义也是我所喜欢的，如果两者不能都有，便牺牲生命，而要道义。

【英译】Fish is what I desire, and bear's paw is also what I desire; if I can not have both, I will give up fish and take bear's paw. Life is what I desire, and righteousness is also what I desire; if I can not have both, I will give up life for righteousness.

52.【原文】有诸内，必形诸外。　　《孟子·告子章句下》

【今译】心里存有什么，一定表现在外。

【英译】What is inside will surely be shown outside.

53.【原文】故天将降大任于是人也，必先苦其心志，劳其筋骨，饿其体肤，空乏其身，行拂乱其所为，所以动心忍性，曾益其所不能。人恒过，然后能改；困于心，衡于虑，而后作；征于色，发于声，而后喻。入则无法家拂士，出则无敌国外患者，国恒亡。然后知生于忧患而死于安乐也。　　《孟子·告子章句下》

【今译】所以上天将要把重大任务落到某人身上，一定先要困苦他的心意，劳累他的筋骨，饥饿他的躯体，穷乏他的身家，使他的每一行为总是不能如意，这样，便可以激励他的心志，坚韧他的性情，增加他的能力。一个人，错误常常发生，才能改正；心意困辱，思虑阻塞，才能有所奋发进而创造；表现在面色上，发表在言语中，才能被人了解。一个国家，如果国内没有守法度的大臣和辅弼的贤士，国外没有相与抗衡的邻国和外来的忧患，常常容易灭亡。这样，就可以知道，忧患的环境足以使人生存、安乐的环境足以使人死亡的道理了。

【英译】So when heaven is about to place great responsibility upon a man, it will first temper his heart and mind, fatigue his bones and muscles with toil, starve him, reduce him to utter destitution and frustrate him in all his attempts so as to stir him up, strengthen his character and develop his capabilities. A man inevitably errs, but only when he has often made mistakes will he correct them. In the same way, only when one is distressed at heart and baffled in mind will he be aroused to creative activities. Only when his feelings and thoughts are shown in his looks and expressed in words can he be understood. If a state has no law-abiding families or wise counselors within and no threat of enemy invasions without, it will perish. Then we will come to know that one survives in worries and miseries and perishes in ease and comfort.

54. 【原文】穷则独善其身，达则兼善天下。　　　　　　　　　　《孟子·尽心章句上》

【今译】贫困时便独自修养自己身心，得意时便使天下之人都受到好处。

【英译】When poor, they tried to better their own condition. When in power, they tried to better the condition of the whole world as well.

55. 【原文】无为其所不为，无欲其所不欲。　　　　　　　　　　《孟子·尽心章句上》

【今译】不干我所不愿干之事，不要我所不愿要之物。

【英译】Do not do what you do not want to do. Do not desire what you choose not to desire.

56. 【原文】孔子登东山而小鲁，登泰山而小天下，故观于海者难于水，游于圣人之门者难为言。　　　　　　　　　　《孟子·尽心章句上》

【今译】孔子登上了东山，便觉得鲁国很小了；登上了泰山，便觉得天下也不大了；所以看过海洋的人，别的水便难以吸引他了；曾在圣人门下学习过的人，别的议论也就难以吸引他了。

【英译】When standing on the top of the Eastern Mountain, Confucius thought the State of Lu very small. When standing on Mount Tai, he thought the whole world small. It is difficult for the sight of a river to satisfy those who have seen the sea, and it is difficult for words to satisfy those who have learned from sages.

57. 【原文】亲亲而仁民，仁民而爱物。　　　　　　　　　　《孟子·尽心章句上》

【今译】君子由亲爱自己的亲人，进而仁爱百姓；由仁爱百姓，进而爱惜万物。

【英译】A gentleman is affectionate to his parents and relatives, so he is benevolent to the people. He is benevolent to the people, so he is careful with things.

58. 【原文】仁者以其所爱及其所不爱，不仁者以其所不爱及其所爱。

《孟子·尽心章句下》

【今译】仁德的人把他所喜爱的，推及他所不喜爱的人；不仁德的人却把他所不喜爱的，推及他所爱的人。

【英译】A benevolent man extends his love from those dear to him to those he does not love. A cruel man extends his cruelty from those who mean nothing to him to those he loves.

59. 【原文】尽信《书》，则不如无《书》。　　　　　　　　　　《孟子·尽心章句下》

【今译】完全相信《书》，还不如没有《书》。

【英译】If everything in *The Book of History* was believed, it would be better for the book not to have been written at all.

60. 【原文】好名之人，能让千乘之国，苟非其人，箪食豆羹见于色。《孟子·尽心章句下》

【今译】喜好名声的人，可以把拥有千辆兵车的大国让给别人，但是，若不是那种值得受让的人，就是要他让一筐饭、一碗汤，那不高兴的神色也会在脸上表现出来。

【英译】A man who seeks after fame can give away a state of a thousand chariots in order to win a good reputation; but if the recipient of his favor is not the right man to serve his purpose, his reluctance will manifest itself on his face even if he is to give away a basketful of rice and a bowlful of soup.

61. 【原文】孟子曰："民为贵，社稷次之，君为轻。" 《孟子·尽心章句下》

【今译】孟子说："百姓最为重要，国家在其次，君主是最轻的。"

【英译】"Of the first importance, " Mencius said, "are the people, next comes the good of land and grains, and of the least importance is the ruler. "

62. 【原文】贤者以其昭昭使人昭昭，今以其昏昏使人昭昭。 《孟子·尽心章句下》

【今译】古时的贤人教导别人，必先使自己彻底明白了，然后才去使别人明白；今天的人教导别人，自己还模模糊糊，却要去使别人明白。

【英译】A man of virtue helps others understand by his own thorough understanding. Nowadays men try to help others understand by their own hazy understanding.

63. 【原文】人皆有所不忍，达之于其所忍，仁也；人皆有所不为，达之于其所为，义也。

《孟子·尽心章句下》

【今译】人人都有不忍心干的事，把它推广到所忍心要干的事上，便是仁；人人都有不肯干的事，把它推广到所肯干的事上，便是义。

【英译】For everyone there are things that he can not bear to see or to do. To have that sentiment also in what he can bring himself to do is benevolence. For everyone there are things that he is not willing to do. To apply that attitude also to what he does is righteousness.

64. 【原文】言近而指远者，善言也；守约而施博者，善道也。 《孟子·尽心章句下》

【今译】言语浅近，意义却深远的，这是"善言"；所坚持的简单，效果却博大的，这是"善道"。

【英译】Words plain and simple but of far-reaching significance are good words. The way of keeping to the pithy but achieving a wide-spread effect is a good way.

65. 【原文】养心莫善于寡欲。 《孟子·尽心章句下》

【今译】修养心性的方法，最好是减少物欲。

【英译】For the cultivation of the heart there is nothing better than to have few desires.

《庄子》
Zhuangzi

【简介】《庄子》是战国早期庄子及后来的学者所著。其文构思巧妙，具有极强的浪漫主义风格，表现出庄子"天人合一"和"清静无为"的思想。庄子，姓庄，名周，字子休，又称子沐，宋国人，所生活的年代约在公元前369年至公元前286年，是战国中期著名的思想家、哲学家和文学家。他继承和发展老子"道法自然"的观点，创立了华夏重要的哲学学派——庄学，为道家学派的主要代表人物之一。

【Introduction】 Zhuangzi was written in the early phase of the Warring States period by Zhuangzi and other scholars. The book with the romantic feature which is full of the wonders of imagination and subtle conceptions expresses the author's theory that man is an integral part of nature and quietism. Zhuangzi(c.369~286 BC) named Zhou, alias Zixiu or Zimu, is a native of Song. He is an important thinker, philosopher and writer in the middle of the Warring States period. He who inherited and developed Laozi's theory "imitation of nature" founded the Zhuang school and is a key representative of the Taoism.

1. 【原文】至人无己，神人无功，圣人无名。 《庄子·逍遥游》

   【今译】道德修养高尚的"至人"能够达到忘我的境界，精神超脱物外的"神人"心目中没有功名利禄，思想修养完美的"圣人"从不追求名誉和地位。

   【英译】The perfect man cares for no Self; the holy man cares for no merits; the sage cares for no fame.

2. 【原文】无为为之之谓天，无为言之之谓德，爱人利物之谓仁，不同同之之谓大，行不崖异之谓宽，有万不同之谓富。 《庄子·天地》

   【今译】用无为的态度去处世就是道，用无为的态度去表达就是德，给人以爱、给物以利就是仁，能包容不同就是大，行为不标新立异就是宽容，能包罗万象就是富有。

   【英译】To act by doing nothing is called the way of heaven; to speak by saying nothing is called virtue; to love people and benefit things is called humanity; to tolerate differences is called greatness; to behave without ostentation is called generosity; to embrace varieties of things is called wealth.

3. 【原文】彼至正者，不失其性命之情。 《庄子·骈拇》

【今译】那所谓的至理正道，就是不违背自然所赋予的事物的本性。

【英译】The so-called proper way is not to deviate from the essence of the inborn nature and the predestined fate.

4. 【原文】天下莫不以物易其性矣。小人则以身殉利，士则以身殉名，大夫则以身殉家，圣人则以身殉天下。 《庄子·骈拇》

【今译】天下没有谁不因为外物而改变自身的本性。平民百姓为了私利而牺牲自己，士人为了名声而牺牲自己，大夫为了家族而牺牲自己，圣人则为了天下而牺牲自己。

【英译】Everyone in the world has been affected by external things and thus has changed his inborn nature. The common people sacrifice themselves for the sake of personal gain; the scholars sacrifice themselves for the sake of fame; the officials sacrifice themselves for the sake of the family; the sages sacrifice themselves for the sake of the state.

5. 【原文】吾所谓臧者，非所谓仁义之谓也，任其性命之情而已矣。 《庄子·骈拇》

【今译】我所说的完善，绝不是所谓的仁义，只是放任天性、保持真性情罢了。

【英译】What I would call perfect is not the so-called humanity and justice, but the indulgence of the inborn nature and maintenance of true feelings.

6. 【原文】知穷之有命，知通之有时，临大难而不惧者，圣人之勇也。 《庄子·秋水》

【今译】知道困顿是因为命运，知道通达是由于时势，面临大难而不畏惧，这就是圣人之勇。

【英译】To know that misfortune is because of destiny and fortune is because of luck, not to show fear in front of great trouble—these manifest the courage of the sages.

7. 【原文】不以心捐道，不以人助天，是之谓真人。 《庄子·大宗师》

【今译】不用心智去损害大道，也不用人为的因素去辅助自然，这就叫"真人"。

【英译】Never impair Tao with the mind and never assist heaven with human efforts. This is what the true man is like.

8. 【原文】圣人法天贵真，不拘于俗。 《庄子·渔夫》

【今译】圣人总是效法自然看重本真，不受世俗的拘束。

【英译】The sage always follows nature, cherishes simplicity and is free of worldly strains.

9. 【原文】今世俗之君子，多危身弃生以殉物，岂不悲哉。 《庄子·让王》

【今译】现在世俗所谓的君子，大多危害身体、弃置生命而一味地追逐身外之物，这难道不可悲吗？

【英译】Nowadays the so-called gentlemen in the earthly world have endangered their health and sacrificed their lives in pursuit of external things. Isn't it lamentable?

10. 【原文】达生之情者，不务生之所无以为；达命之情者，不务知之所无奈何。

《庄子·达生》

【今译】通晓生命真正意义的人，不会去追求生命所不必要的东西；洞悉命运之理的人，不会去追求命运无可奈何的事情。

【英译】Those who understand the essence of life do not seek after what is beyond the reach of life; those who understand the essence of destiny do not seek after what is beyond the power of destiny.

11. 【原文】同则无好也，化则无常也，而果其贤乎！　　　　《庄子·大宗师》

【今译】与万物同一就没有偏私，顺应变化就不固执，你果真成了贤人啊！

【英译】When you are in harmony with everything on earth, you will have no partiality. When you are in accordance with the changes in the world, you will be free from obstinacy. Then you will be a real sage.

12. 【原文】夫欲免为形者，莫如弃世。弃世则无累，无累则正平，正平则与彼更生，更生则几矣。

《庄子·达生》

【今译】想要免于为形体劳累的人，不如舍弃俗世。舍弃俗世就没有劳苦，没有劳苦就心平气和，心平气和就能和自然一起变化更新，跟自然一起变化更新也就接近于大道了。

【英译】He who wants to get rid of physical labor had better abandon earthly affairs. Without earthly affairs, there will be no physical labor. Without physical labor, he will be able to keep a peaceful mind. With the peaceful mind, he will be able to evolve with nature. Being able to evolve with nature, he will be able to get close to Tao.

13. 【原文】夫大道不称，大辩不言，大仁不仁，大廉不嗛，大勇不忮。《庄子·齐物论》

【今译】真正的道是无法说明的，最了不起的辩说是不用言说的，真正的仁爱是不必向人表示仁爱的，真正的廉洁是不必表示谦让的，真正的勇敢是从不伤害他人的。

【英译】The true Tao goes beyond description; the true argument goes beyond words; the true humaneness goes beyond modesty; the true prosperity goes beyond modesty; the true courage goes beyond violence.

14. 【原文】夫道不欲杂，杂则多，多则扰，扰则忧，忧而不救。　　《庄子·人间世》

【今译】推行大道不宜繁杂，繁杂了就会多事，多事就会受到烦扰，烦扰就会引起忧患，忧患到来时就不可挽救了。

【英译】In publicizing Tao, you should avoid being complicated, otherwise there may be excessive matters to attend to, and the excessive matters may cause disturbance, and disturbance will lead to suffering, and then the case will be helpless.

15. 【原文】死生亦大矣，而无变乎己，况爵禄乎！　　　　　　　　　　　《庄子·田子方》

    【今译】死与生也算得上是大事了，却不能使圣人有什么改变，更何况爵位与俸禄呢？

    【英译】Life and death, important as they are, could not affect the sages. Let alone rank and stipend!

16. 【原文】贵富显严名利六者，勃志也。容动色理气意六者，谬心也。《庄子·庚桑楚》

    【今译】高贵、富有、尊显、威严、声明、利禄六项，是扰乱意志的因素。容貌、举止、美色、情理、辞气、意志六项，是束缚心灵的因素。

    【英译】Eminence, wealth, distinction, prestige, fame and profit are the six elements that disturb your will. Appearances, manners, beauty, reason, temperament and attitudes are the six elements that bind your heart.

17. 【原文】礼者，世俗之所为也；真者，所以受于天也，自然不可易也。《庄子·渔父》

    【今译】礼仪，是世俗人的行为；纯真，却是禀受于自然，出自自然因而也就不可改变。

    【英译】Following the rituals is the conduct of the worldly man; purity and innocence is the natural disposition, and accordingly not changeable.

18. 【原文】以德分人谓之圣，以财分人谓之贤。　　　　　　　　　　《庄子·徐无鬼》

    【今译】能用道德去感化他人的人称作圣人，能用财物去周济他人的人称作贤人。

    【英译】He who shares his virtue with others is called a sage and he who shares his property with others is called a worthy man.

19. 【原文】古之真人，以天待人，不以人入天。　　　　　　　　　　《庄子·徐无鬼》

    【今译】古时候的真人，用顺其自然的态度对待人事，不会用人事干扰自然。

    【英译】The true men in ancient times dealt with earthly affairs with a natural attitude and never disturbed nature with earthly affairs.

20. 【原文】至礼有不人，至义不物，至知不谋，至仁无亲，至信辟金。《庄子·庚桑楚》

    【今译】最好的礼仪没有人我之分，最好的道义没有物我之分，最高的智慧不用谋略，最大的仁爱不分亲疏，最大的诚信不用金钱做凭证。

    【英译】The best ritual is to have no distinction between Self and others; the best righteousness is to have no distinction between Self and things; the highest intelligence is not to use schemes; the greatest love is not to be expressed; the greatest faithfulness is not to use money as credence.

21. 【原文】此皆就其利，辞其害，而天下称贤焉。　　　　　　　　　　《庄子·盗跖》

    【今译】这些人都能选取对他们有利的东西，舍弃对他们有害的东西，因而普天下的人们称赞他们是贤明的人。

【英译】They took what was good for them and rejected what was bad for them. Therefore, they were considered as men of virtue and intelligence by people in the world.

22. 【原文】天下大器也，而不以易生，此有道者之所以异乎俗者也。　　《庄子·让王》

    【今译】天下是最为贵重的了，可是却不用它来换取生命，这就是有道之人对待天下跟世俗人大不一样的地方。

    【英译】The throne is most valuable in the world, but it should not substitute life. This is the difference between the people endowed with Tao and the earthly people in their attitude towards power.

23. 【原文】孝子不谀其亲，忠臣不谄其君，臣子之盛也。　　《庄子·天地》

    【今译】孝子不奉承他的父母，忠臣不谄媚他的国君，这是忠臣、孝子尽忠、尽孝的极点。

    【英译】A filial son does not fawn upon his parents and a loyal minister does not flatter his lord. This is the best for the loyal ministers and filial sons.

24. 【原文】通于天下者，德也；行于万物者，道也；上治人者，事也；能有所艺者，技也。

    《庄子·天地》

    【今译】贯穿于天地的是顺应自然的"德"，通行于万物的是听任自然的"道"，善于治理天下的是各尽其能、各任其事，能够让能力和才干充分发挥的是各种技巧。

    【英译】What links the heaven and the earth is virtue; what acts upon everything in the world is Tao; what makes the state well governed is administrative duties; what brings ability and talents into full play is skill.

25. 【原文】其生若浮，其死若休。　　《庄子·刻意》

    【今译】圣人活着犹如在水面漂浮，死亡犹如疲劳后的休息。

    【英译】For the sage, life is like floating on the water and death is like a rest.

26. 【原文】古之至人，先存诸己而后存诸人。所存于己者未定，何暇至于暴人之所行！

    《庄子·人间世》

    【今译】古时候道德修养高尚的至人，总是先保全自己才去扶助他人。如果不能保全自己，哪里还有时间阻止暴君的暴行呢！

    【英译】The men of perfect virtue in ancient times always took care of themselves before they helped the others. If they could not even take care of themselves, how could they hold back the tyrant?

27. 【原文】德人者，居无思，行无虑，不藏是非美恶。四海之内共利之之谓悦，共给之之谓安。　　《庄子·天地》

    【今译】有德行的人安居时不思索，行动时不谋划，不计较是非美丑。与天下人共同分享利益就感到喜悦，共同施予就感到安乐。

【英译】The man of virtue does not contemplate when he has settled down; he does not design when he takes actions; he does not care about the distinction of right and wrong, or good and evil. To share the benefit with the others in the world is joy for him and to give is his happiness.

28.【原文】圣人不从事于务，不就利，不违害，不喜求，不缘道；无谓有谓，有谓无谓，而游乎尘垢之外。　　　　　　　　　　　　　　　　　　　《庄子·齐物论》

【今译】圣人不从事那些世俗的事务，不追逐私利，不回避灾害，不喜好贪求，不拘泥于道；没说话又好像说了，说了话又好像没有说，而心神遨游于尘俗世界之外。

【英译】The sage is never involved in worldly affairs. He does not try to seek after benefits or avoid harms; he does not take delight in seeking after or blindly clinging to Tao. He says nothing and seems to have said something; he says something and seems to have said nothing. Thus, his soul is able to travel beyond the earthly world.

29.【原文】不忘其所始，不求其所终。受而喜之，忘而复之，是之谓不以心捐道，不以人助天。　　　　　　　　　　　　　　　　　　　　　　　《庄子·大宗师》

【今译】圣人不忘记自己的本原，也不寻求自己的归宿，事情来了就欣然接受，忘掉生死让其复归自然，这就叫作不用心智去损害大道，也不用人为的因素去辅助自然。

【英译】The sage does not forget the origin of his life and does not explore the final destiny of his life. He is pleased to accept what comes into his life and to forget life and death and just let it be. This is what is meant by not impairing Tao with the mind and not assisting the heaven with human efforts.

30.【原文】故执德之谓纪，德成之谓立，循于道之谓备，不以物挫志之谓完。

《庄子·天地》

【今译】所以保持德行就是有纲纪，德行的实践就是有建树，遵循大道就是完备，不因外物而损害心志就是完人。

【英译】Therefore, to persevere in virtue is the principle; to perform virtue is achievement; to follow Tao is completion; not to be affected by external things is perfection.

31.【原文】夫恬淡寂寞虚无无为，此天地之本而道德之质也。　　《庄子·刻意》

【今译】恬淡、寂寞、虚无、无为，这便是天地的本原和道德的本质。

【英译】Indifference, solitude, emptiness and inaction, these are the source of the heaven and earth and the essence of virtue.

32.【原文】故德有所长，而形有所忘。　　　　　　　　　　　《庄子·德充符》

【今译】所以只要有过人的德行，形体上的残疾就会被人们遗忘。

【英译】Therefore, for a man with perfect virtue, his physical defects would be forgotten by the others.

33. 【原文】大巧若拙。 《庄子·胠箧》

　　【今译】最大的智巧就好像是笨拙一样。

　　【英译】The great wisdom seems awkward.

34. 【原文】传其常情，无传其溢言，则几乎全。 《庄子·人世间》

　　【今译】传达人之常情，不要传达过分的话语，那么也就大概可以保全自己了。

　　【英译】Convey the truth and never convey the exaggerated words, and then you can protect yourself from harm.

35. 【原文】唇竭而齿寒。 《庄子·胠箧》

　　【今译】嘴唇没了牙齿就会外露受寒。

　　【英译】Since the lips are gone, the teeth get cold.

36. 【原文】真者，精诚之至也。不精不诚，不能动人。 《庄子·渔父》

　　【今译】本真是精诚的极点。不精不诚，就不能感动人。

　　【英译】The natural disposition is the acme of sincerity. Without sincerity, you will never be able to affect the others.

37. 【原文】君子之交淡若水，小人之交甘若醴。君子淡以亲，小人甘以绝。

《庄子·山木》

　　【今译】君子之间的交情清淡得像水一样，小人之间的交情甘美得像甜酒一样。君子间的交情虽然清淡但是亲切，小人间的交情虽然甘甜却容易断绝。

　　【英译】The relationship between the superior men is as plain as water; the relationship between the inferior men is as luscious as wine. The former is plain but close while the latter is luscious but callous.

38. 【原文】人皆知有用之用，而莫知无用之用也。 《庄子·人间世》

　　【今译】人们都知道有用的用处，却不知道无用的用处。

　　【英译】Everyone knows the benefit of being useful, but does not know the benefit of being useless.

39. 【原文】凡外重者内拙。 《庄子·达生》

　　【今译】凡是对外物看得过重的人，其内心一定笨拙。

　　【英译】Those who pay more attention to external things are clumsy internally.

40. 【原文】死生为昼夜。 《庄子·至乐》

　　【今译】生死就像昼夜一样，属于自然的变化。

　　【英译】The succession of life and death is just like the succession of day and night.

41. 【原文】夫哀莫大于心死，而人死亦次之。 《庄子·田子方》

【今译】最悲哀的莫过于心死，身体的死亡还是次要的。

【英译】No sorrow is greater than the death of the heart. Even the death of the body is next to it.

42.【原文】人生天地之间，若白驹之过隙，忽然而已。　　　　　　　　　《庄子·知北游》

【今译】人生于天地之间，就像小马在细小的缝隙前一闪而过，只是一瞬间而已。

【英译】The life of a man is as brief as the passage of a horse through a gap in a wall.

43.【原文】此木以不材得终其天年。　　　　　　　　　　　　　　　　　《庄子·山木》

【今译】这棵树就是因为不成材而能够终享天年啊！

【英译】This tree can live out its natural life span because it is worthless.

44.【原文】为人使易以伪，为天使难以伪。　　　　　　　　　　　　　　《庄子·人间世》

【今译】被他人所驱使就容易作伪，被天性所驱使就难以作伪。

【英译】It is easy to put on false appearance when compelled by the others; it is hard to put on false appearance when compelled by nature.

45.【原文】名止于实，义设于适。　　　　　　　　　　　　　　　　　　《庄子·至乐》

【今译】名实要符合，义理的设定要适应各自的天性。

【英译】The reputation should be in accordance with the reality and principles should be in accordance with individuality.

46.【原文】直木先伐，甘井先竭。　　　　　　　　　　　　　　　　　　《庄子·山木》

【今译】长得很直的树木总是先被砍伐，甘甜的井水总是先被汲干。

【英译】The trees that are straight get cut down first; the wells that are sweet get drawn dry first.

47.【原文】彼无故以合者，则无故以离。　　　　　　　　　　　　　　　《庄子·山木》

【今译】凡是无缘无故结合在一起的，也就会无缘无故地离散。

【英译】Those who get related to each other for no reason will get separated with no reason.

48.【原文】入其俗，从其令。　　　　　　　　　　　　　　　　　　　　《庄子·山木》

【今译】每到一个地方，就要遵从当地的风俗、政令。

【英译】Wherever you go, follow the local customs and laws.

49.【原文】天地非不广且大也，人之所用容足耳。　　　　　　　　　　　《庄子·外物》

【今译】天地不能说不宽广，但人所用的只是容身之地而已。

【英译】Although the heaven and the earth are vast and broad, what we need is a place where we can put our feet.

50.【原文】美成在久，恶成不及改，可不慎与！　　　　　　　　　　　　《庄子·人间世》

【今译】成就一件好事需要很长时间，做出一件坏事就后悔莫及、难以补救了，为人处世能不谨慎吗？

【英译】To accomplish something good takes a long time, while once you do something wrong, it may be too late to amend. You cannot be too careful!

51. 【原文】察乎安危，宁于福祸，谨于去就，莫之能害也。　　　　　　　　《庄子·秋水》

【今译】善于观察情况的安危，对于幸福和灾祸都能内心平静，无论舍弃还是获取都很谨慎，所以没有什么能伤害他。

【英译】He is good at observing fortune and misfortune, not disturbed by whatever comes to him and prudent in making decisions of abandoning or taking. Therefore, nothing can do harm to him.

52. 【原文】其马力竭矣，而犹求焉，故曰败。　　　　　　　　　　　　　　《庄子·达生》

【今译】马已经筋疲力尽了，还要它奔跑，所以说它会倒下。

【英译】The horse was exhausted, but he kept it galloping. That was why I said it would fall.

53. 【原文】先圣不一而能，不同其事。　　　　　　　　　　　　　　　　　《庄子·至乐》

【今译】古代的圣贤不乞求人们有统一的才能，也不乞求人们做相同的事情。

【英译】The ancient sages did not hope that all the people had the same talent or did the same thing.

54. 【原文】且有大觉而后知此其大梦也，而愚者自以为觉，窃窃然知之。

《庄子·齐物论》

【今译】只有非常清醒觉悟的人才能知道人生就像一场大梦，可愚笨的人却以为自己是清醒的，以为自己明察一切，什么都知道。

【英译】Only the one who is completely awakened can realize that life is just like a grand dream, while the fool thinks that he is awake and aware of everything.

55. 【原文】势为天子而不以贵骄人，富有天下而不以财戏人。　　　　　　　《庄子·盗跖》

【今译】权势高贵为天子，也不应该因为地位高贵而轻视别人。一个人富有天下，也不能以自己的财富戏弄别人。

【英译】Some people may be as powerful as kings, but they will not despise the others because of their positions. Some people may possess as much as a kingdom, but they will not be domineering because of their wealth.

56. 【原文】且子独不闻夫寿陵余子之学行于邯郸与？未得国能，又失其故行矣，直匍匐而归耳。　　　　　　　　　　　　　　　　　　　　　　　《庄子·秋水》

【今译】你难道没听说过寿陵少年去邯郸学步的事吗？他没学到赵国人走路的技巧，

反而忘了自己走路的方法，以至于只能爬着回家。

【英译】Haven't you heard of the story that a young man from Shouling went to Handan to learn their way of walking? He failed to learn how to walk as the people in Handan and forgot his own way of walking. As a result, he had to crawl home.

57.【原文】处势不便，未足以逞其能也。　　　　　　　　　　　　　　《庄子·山木》

【今译】处在不利的情势下，就不能充分施展才能。

【英译】When a person is in an unfavorable situation, he cannot bring his competence into full play.

58.【原文】好面誉人者，亦好背而毁之。　　　　　　　　　　　　　　《庄子·盗跖》

【今译】好当面夸奖别人的人，也好背地里诋毁别人。

【英译】Those who praise somebody to his face are likely to smear him behind his back.

59.【原文】施于人而不忘，非天布也。　　　　　　　　　　　　　　《庄子·列御寇》

【今译】给予别人恩惠却总忘不了让人回报，这远不是自然对天下广泛而无私的赐予。

【英译】Doing a favor for the others with the intention of receiving rewards is not a favor at all.

60.【原文】凡人心险于山川，难于知天。　　　　　　　　　　　　　　《庄子·列御寇》

【今译】人心比山川还要险恶，了解人心比预测天象还要困难。

【英译】The human mind is more tricky than steep cliffs. Understanding the human mind is more difficult than predicting the weather.

61.【原文】功成之美，无一其迹矣。事亲以适，不论所以矣；饮酒以乐，不选其具矣；处丧以哀，无问其礼矣。　　　　　　　　　　　　　　《庄子·渔夫》

【今译】功业的成就在于完美，不必拘于一定的途径。侍奉双亲是为了让他们感到安适，不必考虑为什么；饮酒是为了欢乐，没有必要选择酒菜和餐具；居丧是为了表达哀伤，不必讲究规范和礼仪。

【英译】The end justifies the means, so there are various ways of achieving the purpose. Waiting on the parents is to make them feel comfortable and there is no need to worry about the means. Drinking is for happiness and there is no need to care about the dishes and tableware. Holding a funeral is to express the grief and there is no need to pay attention to rituals.

62.【原文】天地之养一也，登高不可以为长，居下不可以为短。　　　　《庄子·徐无鬼》

【今译】天地养育万物是一视同仁的，登上了高位不可自以为尊贵，身处低下的地位也不可自以为卑贱。

【英译】The heaven and the earth provide the same nourishment to everything in the world.

There is nothing to be proud of for being in the high position and there is no need to feel inferior for being in the low position.

63. 【原文】戒之哉！嗟乎！无以汝色骄人哉！ 《庄子·徐无鬼》

   【今译】警惕啊！千万不要用高傲的态度对待别人啊！

   【英译】Take it as a warning! Never treat the others arrogantly!

64. 【原文】狗不以善吠为良，人不以善言为贤。 《庄子·徐无鬼》

   【今译】狗不因为能叫便是好狗，人不因为会说话便是贤能的人。

   【英译】A barking dog is not necessarily dutiful; a talktive person is not always sage.

65. 【原文】鸟兽不厌高，鱼鳖不厌深。夫全其形生之人，藏其身也，不厌深渺而已矣。

   《庄子·庚桑楚》

   【今译】鸟兽不满足高飞，鱼鳖不满足水深。那些保全身体和本性的人要隐藏自己，也是不满足深幽高远罢了。

   【英译】Therefore, the birds and beasts do not mind how high the mountain is and the fish and turtles do not mind how deep the water is. Those who want to remain safe and conceal themselves do not mind how remote and reclusive they live.

66. 【原文】不能容人者无亲，无亲者尽人。 《庄子·庚桑楚》

   【今译】不能容人的人没有人亲近，没有人亲近的人也就为人们所弃绝。

   【英译】He who cannot tolerate the others will have no friend close to him. He who has no friend close to him will be abandoned by the others.

67. 【原文】势为天子，未必贵也；穷为匹夫，未必贱也。贵贱之分，在行之美恶。

   《庄子·盗跖》

   【今译】权势大如天子，未必尊贵；穷困为贫民，未必卑贱。贵贱的分别在于品行的美恶好坏。

   【英译】Someone as powerful as the king may not be noble or superior, and someone as poor as a pauper may not be humble or inferior. The distinction of nobility and humbleness lies in the virtue.

68. 【原文】泉涸，鱼相与处于陆，相呴以湿，相濡以沫，不如相忘于江湖。

   《庄子·天运》

   【今译】泉水干涸了，鱼儿相互依偎在陆地上，靠大口出气来取得一点儿湿气，靠唾沫来相互湿润，却不如在江湖里彼此相忘。

   【英译】When the springs dry up, the fish are stranded on the land, moistening each other with their breath and damping each other with their slime. But it would be much better for them to live in the rivers or lakes and forget each other.

69. 【原文】平为福，有余为害者，物莫不然，而财其甚。 　　　　　《庄子·盗跖》

【今译】拥有的东西达到平均水平是福气，有余就是祸害，凡是事物没有不是这样的，而财物尤其突出。

【英译】Average possession means happiness; surplus means trouble. This applies to all and it is even so with material acquisition.

70. 【原文】灾人者，人必反灾之。 　　　　　《庄子·人间世》

【今译】加害别人的人，别人必定反过来害他。

【英译】Those who do harmful things to the others will be harmed by someone else in turn.

71. 【原文】自伐者无功；功成者堕，名成者亏。 　　　　　《庄子·山木》

【今译】自己夸耀的人反而没有功绩；功业成功而不知退隐的人必定会毁败，名声彰显而不知韬光养晦的人必定会遭到损伤。

【英译】He who is conceited will not accomplish anything; he who does not retire after his accomplishment will come to ruin; he who rests on his fame will suffer from losses.

72. 【原文】荣辱立，然后睹所病；货财聚，然后睹所争。 　　　　　《庄子·则阳》

【今译】世间有了荣辱的区别，各种弊端就显示出来了；财货日渐聚积，然后各种争斗就表露出来了。

【英译】When honor and disgrace is well defined, malpractices come into being; when wealth is accumulated, disputes begin to appear.

73. 【原文】可乎可，不可乎不可。道行之而成，物谓之而然。 　　　　　《庄子·齐物论》

【今译】世界上可以做的事情有可以做的理由，不可以做的事情有不可以做的理由。道路是人们走出来的，事物的名字是人们叫出来的。

【英译】There are reasons for doing something and not doing something. A path is formed because we walk on it; a thing has a name because we call it so.

74. 【原文】不利货财，不近贵富；不乐寿，不哀夭；不荣通，不丑穷。 　　《庄子·天地》

【今译】不谋财货，不求富贵；不把长寿看作快乐，不把夭折看作悲哀；不把通达看作荣耀，不把穷困看作羞耻。

【英译】He does not seek property or pursue wealth; he does not regard longevity as happiness or premature death as misfortune; he does not regard high rank as honor or poverty as shame.

75. 【原文】至人之用心若镜，不将不迎，应而不藏，故能胜物而不伤。《庄子·应帝王》

【今译】"至人"的心思就像一面镜子，对于外物的来去不迎不送，如实反映事物本身而无所隐藏，所以能够反映外物而不为外物所损伤。

【英译】The perfect person has a mind like a mirror, which neither welcomes nor sends things from outside, which reflects things without concealing. Therefore, it can reflect things from outside without getting harmed.

76. 【原文】行乎无名者，唯庸有光。　　　　　　　　　　　　《庄子·庚桑楚》

   【今译】行事不显露名声的人，即使平庸也有光彩。

   【英译】He who acts without caring about fame may be plain but brilliant.

77. 【原文】正则静，静则明，明则虚，虚则无为而无不为也。　　《庄子·庚桑楚》

   【今译】内心平正就会宁静，宁静就会明澈，明澈就会空明，空明就能顺其自然而没有什么做不成的。

   【英译】If you are peaceful in mind, you will enjoy serenity; if you can enjoy serenity, you will be clear in mind; if you are clear in mind, you will enjoy emptiness; if you can enjoy emptiness, you can follow the course of nature and there is nothing you cannot achieve.

78. 【原文】宇泰定者，发乎天光。　　　　　　　　　　　　　　《庄子·庚桑楚》

   【今译】心境安泰镇定的人，就会发出自然的光辉。

   【英译】He who has a peaceful mind radiates divine light.

79. 【原文】知道者必达于理，达于理者必明于权，明于权者不以物害己。《庄子·秋水》

   【今译】懂得大道理的人必定通达事理，通达事理的人必定能随机应变，明白应变的人定然不会因为外物而损伤自己。

   【英译】Those who are aware of Tao are surely able to understand reasoning; those who understand reasoning are surely able to adapt themselves to the situation; those who can adapt themselves to the situation will not get harmed by external things.

80. 【原文】圣人安其所安，不安其所不安；众人安其所不安，不安其所安。

   《庄子·列御寇》

   【今译】圣人安于自然，却不适应人为的摆布；普通人习惯于人为的摆布，却不安于自然。

   【英译】Sages who are content with the natural state of things are not willing to be ordered about by conscious manipulations; common people who are accustomed to being ordered about do not feel at ease with the natural state of things.

81. 【原文】纯粹而不杂，静一而不变，淡而无为，动而以天行，此养神之道也。

   《庄子·刻意》

   【今译】单纯精粹而不混杂，虚静专一而不变动，恬淡无为，行动顺应自然，这就是养神的道理和方法。

   【英译】Purity without diversion, concentration without wavering, indifference without action and movement in accordance with nature—these are the essence of spiritual maintenance.

82. 【原文】汝为知在毫毛，而不知大宁。 《庄子·列御寇》

【今译】世俗人把心思用在赐赠酬答等琐碎的小事上，却一点也不懂得宁静、自然和无为。

【英译】Secular people spend a good deal of time and energy on trifling matters, but know nothing about serenity and nature.

83. 【原文】绝圣弃知而天下大治。 《庄子·在宥》

【今译】弃绝聪明智巧，天下就会得到治理而太平无事。

【英译】If we abandon wisdom and intelligence, the world will be well governed and peaceful.

84. 【原文】至德之世，不尚贤，不使能；上如标枝，民如野鹿。 《庄子·天地》

【今译】盛德的时代，不标榜贤能，不崇尚技巧；国君如同居于高位，百姓如野鹿一样无拘无束，自由自在。

【英译】In the times when virtue prevails, the talented are not honored and skills are not valued. The rulers are as modest as the upper branches of trees and the people are as free as wild deer.

85. 【原文】圣人之用兵也，亡国而不失人心。 《庄子·大宗师》

【今译】古代的圣人使用武力，灭掉敌国却不失掉敌国的民心。

【英译】Therefore, when the sage wages a war, he can conquer a state without losing the support of its people.

86. 【原文】故贵以身于为天下，则可以托天下；爱以身于为天下，则可以寄天下。

《庄子·在宥》

【今译】以尊重自身生命甚于尊重天下的态度治理天下的人，才可以把天下托付给他；以珍爱自身生命甚于珍爱天下的态度去治理天下的人，才可以把天下托付给他。

【英译】He who treasures his state as he does his own life can be entrusted with governing his state; he who loves his state as he does his own life can be entrusted with governing his state.

87. 【原文】庶人有旦暮之业则劝，百工有器械之巧则壮。 《庄子·徐无鬼》

【今译】百姓只要有短暂的工作就会勤勉，工匠只要有器械的技巧就会气壮。

【英译】The common people will work industriously if they are busy from morning till night; the artisans will be full of energy if they are skilled with their tools.

88. 【原文】古之君人者，以得为在民，以失为在己。 《庄子·则阳》

【今译】古代治理国家的人，把功绩归于百姓，把过失归于自己。

【英译】The ancient rulers attributed success to the people and attributed failure to themselves.

89. 【原文】君子不为苛察。 《庄子·天下》

【今译】君子不对他人求全责备，吹毛求疵。

【英译】The men of virtue never make excessive demands on the others.

90. 【原文】夫有土者，有大物也。有大物者，不可以物；物而不物，故能物物。

《庄子·在宥》

【今译】拥有国家的，就拥有土地人民。拥有土地人民的，不可以受外物支配；支配外物而不为外物所役使，才能够主宰万物。

【英译】The one who owns a state owns the land and the people. The one who owns the land and the people should not be influenced by worldly things. Only the one who dominates the world and is not influenced by it can govern everything in the world.

91. 【原文】唯无以天下为者，可以托天下也。 《庄子·让王》

【今译】只有不以天下为自己所用的人，才可以把统治天下的重任托付给他。

【英译】Only he who does not want to rule over the state can be entrusted with the throne.

92. 【原文】有治在人，忘乎物，忘乎天，其名为忘己。 《庄子·天地》

【今译】倘若果真存在着什么治理，那也就是人们遵循本性活动，忘掉外物，忘掉自然，它的名字就叫作忘掉自己。

【英译】Governing is to follow the natural instinct of man, if it does exist. To forget external things and forget nature is called to forget the self.

93. 【原文】大知闲闲，小知间间。大言炎炎，小言詹詹。 《庄子·齐物论》

【今译】有大才智的人广博豁达，有点小聪明的人则斤斤计较；合于大道的言论气焰凌人，拘于智巧的言论唠叨不休。

【英译】Men of great wits are open and broad-minded; men of small wits are mean and meticulous. Men in accordance with Tao speak with aggression; men clinging to ingenuity keep on nagging.

94. 【原文】日凿一窍，七日而浑沌死。 《庄子·应帝王》

【今译】每天为混沌造出一个孔窍，凿了七天混沌就死去了。（混沌是原始纯朴的人民的象征）

【英译】They chiseled an aperture everyday and on the seventh day Chaos died. (Chaos stands for the pure ancient people)

95. 【原文】彼其物无穷，而人皆以为有终；彼其物无测，而人皆以为有极。

《庄子·在宥》

【今译】"至道"是没有穷尽的，然而人们却认为有终结；"至道"是不可能探测的，然而人们却认为有极限。

【英译】The "perfection of Tao" is eternal, while the people consider it ephemeral; the "perfection of Tao" is unfathomable, while the people consider it limited.

96. 【原文】吾生也有涯，而知也无涯。以有涯随无涯，殆已；已而为知者，殆而已矣。

《庄子·养生主》

【今译】人们的生命是有限的，而知识却是无限的。以有限的生命去追求无限的知识，势必非常疲惫。既然这样还要不停地追求知识，只能更加疲惫不堪罢了！

【英译】Our life is limited, but knowledge is unlimited. To pursue the unlimited knowledge in the limited life is sure to be fatiguing. To know this but still keep on pursuing is even more fatiguing.

97. 【原文】可以言论者，物之粗也；可以意致者，物之精也。言之所不能论，意之所不能致者，不期精粗焉。

《庄子·秋水》

【今译】可以用言语来谈论的东西，是事物粗浅的表象；可以用心灵来感悟的，则是事物精微的内在本质。既不能用言语谈论，又不能以心意传达的，就不必区分什么精微粗浅了。

【英译】What can be discussed in words is something shallow and superficial; what can be felt with heart is something subtle and substantial. For those that can neither be discussed in words nor felt with heart, there is no need to distinguish whether they are shallow or subtle.

98. 【原文】小知不及大知，小年不及大年。

《庄子·逍遥游》

【今译】小聪明赶不上大智慧，寿命短的不能了解寿命长的。

【英译】Little learning does not come up to great learning; the short-lived does not come up to the long-lived.

99. 【原文】故大知观于远近。

《庄子·秋水》

【今译】所以具有大智慧的人观察事物从不局限于一个方面、一个部分。

【英译】Therefore, the man of great intelligence observes things from far and near.

100. 【原文】夫知者不言，言者不知，故圣人行不言之教。

《庄子·知北游》

【今译】道"道"的人不说，说的人并不是真知道"道"，所以圣人施行的是不靠说教的教导。

【英译】Those who know never say and those who say never know. Therefore, the sage teaches without words.

101. 【原文】故知止其所不知，至矣；若有不即是者，天钧败之。

《庄子·齐物论》

【今译】知识的探求停止于他所不能知晓的境域，就是极点了；如果不这样，自然的本性就要遭到亏损。

【英译】It is the acme if the quest for knowledge stops where one does not know; if not so, the natural self will be damaged.

102. 【原文】道隐于小成，言隐于荣华。 《庄子·齐物论》
    【今译】大道被小小的成就所隐蔽，言论被浮华的辞藻所掩盖。
    【英译】Tao is obscured when it is concealed by minor achievements; speech is obscured when it is concealed by flowery words.

103. 【原文】欲是其所非而非其所是，则莫若以明。 《庄子·齐物论》
    【今译】想要肯定对方所否定的东西而非难对方所肯定的东西，那么不如用澄明的心境去观察事物的本相。
    【英译】To approve what the other disapproves and disapprove what the other approves is no better than to observe with a tranquil mind.

104. 【原文】知天之所为，知人之所为者，至矣。 《庄子·大宗师》
    【今译】知道什么是自然的，知道什么是人为的，这就是智慧的最高境界了。
    【英译】To know what the heaven can do and to know what man can do is the perfection of wisdom.

105. 【原文】古之存身者，不以辩饰知，不以知穷天下，不以知穷德。 《庄子·缮性》
    【今译】古时讲究存身之道的人，不用辩说来巧饰智慧，不用智慧来困扰天下人，不用智慧来困扰德行。
    【英译】Those who preserved themselves in ancient times did not ornament their intelligence with eloquence; they did not disturb the others with their intelligence; they did not confuse virtue with wisdom.

106. 【原文】博之不必知，辩之不必慧。 《庄子·知北游》
    【今译】博学的人不一定具有智慧，善于辩论的人不一定聪明。
    【英译】The well-read man is not necessarily learned; an eloquent man is not necessarily intelligent.

107. 【原文】不知深矣，知之浅矣；弗知内矣，知之外矣。 《庄子·知北游》
    【今译】说不知道的是深奥，说知道的则是浅薄；说不知道的是内行，说知道的才是外行。
    【英译】Ignorance is profound and knowledge is shallow. Ignorance reaches the essence of Tao and knowledge is but superficial.

108. 【原文】虽有至知，万人谋之。 《庄子·外物》
    【今译】一个人虽然有很高的智慧，也怕众人一起打他的主意。
    【英译】Perfect wisdom can be outwitted by ten thousand schemes.

109. 【原文】无藏逆于得，无以巧胜人，无以谋胜人，无以战胜人。 《庄子·徐无鬼》

【今译】不要背理贪求，不要用巧诈去战胜别人，不要用谋略去战胜别人，不要用战争去征服别人。

【英译】Never lust for gains against reason, or conquer the others with deception, scheme or armed forces.

110.【原文】注焉而不满，酌焉而不竭，而不知其所由来，此之谓葆光。《庄子·齐物论》

【今译】怎么倾注也装不满，怎么汲取也取不尽，而不知其来源，这就叫作隐藏它的光辉。

【英译】Pour into it and it will never fill; dip from it and it will never dry. You will never know where it comes. This is called the preserved light.

111.【原文】知与恬交相养，而和理出其性。　　　　　　　　　　《庄子·缮性》

【今译】才智与恬淡的性情相互保养，道德便在心中形成了。

【英译】When wisdom and tranquility nurture each other, virtue is formed in the heart.

112.【原文】知有所困，神有所不及也。　　　　　　　　　　　　《庄子·外物》

【今译】机智也有困穷的时候，即使神灵也会有始料不及的事情。

【英译】Wisdom has its limit and even the gods have things beyond their power.

113.【原文】知者之所不知，犹睨也。　　　　　　　　　　　　《庄子·庚桑楚》

【今译】具有智慧的人也会有不了解的知识，就像斜视一方，所看见的必定有局限。

【英译】Even those who are intelligent have something that they do not know. It is just like that what is seen is limited when looking at one side only.

114.【原文】是故丘山积卑而为高，江河合水而为大，大人并合而为公。《庄子·则阳》

【今译】所以说山丘积聚卑小的土石才成就其高，江河汇聚细流才成就其大，伟大的人物并合了众人的意见才成就其公。

【英译】Therefore, the mountains are high when the small stones accumulate; the rivers are large when the small streams accumulate; the great men are accomplished when the others' traits accumulate.

115.【原文】大惑者，终身不解；大愚者，终身不灵。　　　　　　《庄子·天地》

【今译】大迷惑的人，终身不能觉悟；大愚昧的人，终身不知道自己愚昧。

【英译】Those who are in the worst confusion will never get rid of the confusion for their entire lives; those who are the worst fools will never realize it for their entire lives.

116.【原文】井蛙不可以语于海者，拘于虚也；夏虫不可以语于冰者，笃于时也；曲士不可以语于道者，束于教也。　　　　　　　　　　　　　　　　《庄子·秋水》

【今译】井里的青蛙，不可能跟它谈论大海，是因为受到生活空间的限制；夏天的虫子，不可能跟它谈论冰霜，是因为受到时间的限制；乡下的书生，不能和他谈论大道理，是因为他受了礼教的束缚。

【英译】You cannot talk about the sea with a frog in the well, because it is confined to its dwelling place; you cannot talk about frost with a summer worm, because it is limited to the season; you cannot talk about Tao with a rural scholar, because he is restrained to the rites.

117.【原文】言者所以在意，得意而忘言。　　　　　　　　　　　《庄子·外物》

【今译】言语是用来表达真意的，领会了真意就忘掉了言语。

【英译】Words are used to convey meaning. When the meaning is comprehended, the words are forgotten.

118.【原文】夫道，覆载万物者也，洋洋乎大哉！　　　　　　　　《庄子·天地》

【今译】道，是覆盖万物的，浩瀚广大！

【英译】Tao covers everything in the world. How magnificent it is!

119.【原文】道不可有，有不可无。道之为名，所假而行。　　　　《庄子·则阳》

【今译】道不能执着于有形，也不能执着于无形。道之所以称作"道"，只不过是借了道的名义而已。

【英译】Tao does not have a form, but Tao is not formless. That Tao is called "Tao" is for the name's sake.

120.【原文】且道者，万物之所由也，庶物失之者死，得之者生。为事逆之则败，顺之则成。

《庄子·渔父》

【今译】道是万物产生的根源，各种事物失去了它，就会死亡；得到了它，就能生存。做事情顺应了它，就能成功；违背了它，就会失败。

【英译】Tao is the source of everything in the world. Without it, everything in the world will perish. With it, everything will flourish. If we do things in accordance with it, we will succeed. If we go against it, we will fail.

121.【原文】天下有常然。常然者，曲者不以钩，直者不以绳，圆者不以规，方者不以矩，附离不以胶漆，约束不以纆索。　　　　　　　　　　　　　　　　《庄子·骈拇》

【今译】天下事物都各有它们固有的常态。所谓常态，就是弯曲的不依靠曲尺，笔直的不依靠墨线，圆的不依靠圆规，方的不依靠角尺，使分离的东西附着在一起不依靠胶和漆，将单个的事物捆束在一起不依靠绳索。

【英译】Everything in the world has its normal state. The so-called normal state is curving without a try square, straight without a ruler, round without a compass, square without an angle square, attached without glue and bound without ropes.

122.【原文】天地与我并生，万物与我为一。　　　　　　　　　　《庄子·齐物论》

【今译】天地与我一起生存，万物与我浑然一体。

【英译】The heaven and the earth and I exist at the same time; all things in the world and I are one uniformity.

123.【原文】不知周之梦为蝴蝶与，蝴蝶之梦为周与？　　　　　　　　《庄子·齐物论》

【今译】庄子梦见蝴蝶，梦醒后，搞不清是庄周梦见了蝴蝶呢，还是蝴蝶梦见了庄周呢？

【英译】He cannot tell whether it was Zhuang Zhou dreamed of the butterfly or the butterfly dreamed of Zhuang Zhou.

124.【原文】天地一指，万物一马。　　　　　　　　　　　　　　　　《庄子·齐物论》

【今译】从事理相同的观点来看，天地只有一种元素，万物纷纷也只是一类。

【英译】Such is the case with heaven and earth and everything in the world, they are just like the case with the finger and the horse—they are the same substance in nature.

125.【原文】万物一府，死生同状。　　　　　　　　　　　　　　　　　《庄子·天地》

【今译】万物最终归结于同一，死与生也并不存在区别。

【英译】Everything in the world will return to the same root, so there is no distinction between life and death.

126.【原文】指穷于为薪，火传也，不知其尽也。　　　　　　　　　　《庄子·养生主》

【今译】蜡烛有烧尽的时候，而火种却世世代代传续下来，永远不会熄灭。

【英译】The candle may be consumed, but the fire will be passed on, and it will never be extinguished.

127.【原文】物无非彼，物无是非。自彼则不见，自知则知之。故曰：彼出于是，是亦因彼。

《庄子·齐物论》

【今译】各种事物无不存在它自身的对立面，各种事物也无不存在它自身的一面。从他方看就看不到这一面，从自身知道的这一面讲当然是知道的。所以说彼产生于此，此也因此依存于彼。

【英译】Everything in the world has its otherness and everything in the world has its selfness. What cannot be seen in otherness can be known from selfness. Therefore, otherness comes from selfness and selfness depends on otherness.

128.【原文】方生方死，方死方生；方可方不可，方不可方可，因是因非，因非因是。

《庄子·齐物论》

【今译】各种事物随起随灭，随灭随起；可以的可以变为不可，不可又可以变为可以；是因非而出现，非因是而产生。

【英译】Where there is birth, there must be death; where there is death, there must be birth.

Possibility may turn to impossibility and impossibility may turn to possibility. The right may lead to the wrong and the wrong may lead to the right.

129. 【原文】穷则反，终则始；此物之所有。　　　　　　　　　　《庄子·则阳》

【今译】物极必反，结束意味着新的开始，这是事物具有的共同规律。

【英译】Everything will turn back when it reaches the limit. The end means the beginning. This is the universal law of everything in the world.

130. 【原文】非彼无我，非我无所去。　　　　　　　　　　　　《庄子·齐物论》

【今译】没有对立面就没有我，没有我对立面我也就无所呈现。

【英译】There is no otherness if there is no selfness, and if there is no otherness, the selfness cannot show itself.

131. 【原文】本在于上，末在于下。　　　　　　　　　　　　　《庄子·天道》

【今译】根本的东西是最重要的，末节的东西则处于不重要的地位。

【英译】The essence is of extreme importance, while the trivial things are less important.

132. 【原文】有天道，有人道。无为而尊者，天道也；有为而累者，人道也。

《庄子·在宥》

【今译】有天道，有人道。无所作为却处于崇高地位的，就是天道；有所作为而劳累困苦的，就是人道。

【英译】There is the Tao of heaven and Tao of humanity. To do nothing and yet enjoy great honor is the Tao of heaven; to do things and toil is the Tao of humanity.

133. 【原文】祸福淳淳，至有所拂者而有所宜。　　　　　　　　《庄子·则阳》

【今译】祸福在不停地流转，出现违逆的一面同时也就存在相宜的一面。

【英译】Fortune and misfortune have their comings and goings. The pros and cons coexist in the same time.

134. 【原文】安危相易，祸福相生，缓急相摩，聚散以成。　　　《庄子·则阳》

【今译】安危相互变易，祸福相互生成，缓急相互交替，聚散因此而形成。

【英译】Safety and danger alternate with each other; fortune and misfortune interchange with each other; relaxation and emergency succeed each other; accumulation and dispersion are formed like this.

135. 【原文】是亦彼也，彼亦是也。彼亦一是非，此亦一是非。　《庄子·齐物论》

【今译】此即是彼，彼即是此，彼也有它的是非，此也有它的是非。

【英译】Selfness is otherness and otherness is selfness. There is right and wrong in otherness and there is right and wrong in selfness.

136. 【原文】不以生生死，不以死死生。死生有待邪？皆有所一体。　《庄子·知北游》

【今译】不是为了生才产生死，也不是为了死才终止生。生和死是相辅相成的对立面吗？生和死都是一体的。

【英译】Death is not generated because of life and life is not stopped because of death. Are life and death opposite to each other? Life and death are closely related.

137.【原文】天无为以之清，地无为以之宁，故两无为相合，万物皆化。《庄子·至乐》

【今译】天无为而自然清虚，地无为而自然宁静，天与地两个无为相互结合，万物就全都变化生长。

【英译】The heaven is clear because it does nothing; the earth is quiet because it does nothing. As neither the heaven nor the earth does anything, everything in the world grows and evolves.

138.【原文】天地者，万物之父母也，合则成体，散则成始。　《庄子·达生》

【今译】天和地，是生养万物的父母，物质元素结合便形成万物的形态，物质元素一旦离散又成为另一物体产生的开始。

【英译】The heaven and the earth give birth to everything in the world. Their combination brings the formation of all the things in the world. Their separation brings the beginning of new things.

139.【原文】天地有大美而不言，四时有明法而不议，万物有成理而不说。

《庄子·知北游》

【今译】天地具有伟大的美德却不言说，四时有明显的法则却不自己表达，万物变化有永恒的规律却不讲出来。

【英译】The heaven and the earth have the highest virtue, but they do not speak a single word. The four seasons occur in regular cycles, but they do not raise a single argument. All things in the world change according to a fixed rule, but they do not give a single explanation.

140.【原文】合则离，成则毁，廉则挫，尊则议，有为则亏，贤则谋，不肖则欺，胡可得而必乎哉。　《庄子·山木》

【今译】有聚合就有离散，有成功就有毁败，锐利就会遭到挫折，尊崇就会遭受议论，有作为就会受亏损，贤能就会被谋算，而无能就会受到欺侮，怎么可以偏滞一方呢！

【英译】Where there is union, there is separation; where there is completion, there is destruction; where there is keenness, there is frustration; where there is honor, there is reproach; where there is accomplishment, there is failure; where there is capability, there is undermining; where there is incapability, there is bullying. How can we look just at the one side?

141.【原文】同类相从，同声相应，固天之理也。　《庄子·渔父》

【今译】事物同类的就互相聚集，同声的就相互应和，本来就是自然的道理。

【英译】Things of the same kind cluster and sounds of the same frequency harmonize. This is the law of nature.

142.【原文】人之生，气之聚也；聚则为生，散则为死。若死生之徒，吾又何患！

《庄子·知北游》

【今译】人的诞生，是气的聚合，气的聚合形成生命，气的离散便是死亡。如果死与生是同类相属的，那么对于死亡我又忧患什么呢？

【英译】 The birth of the man is the accumulation of the vital energy. The accumulation of the vital energy forms life and the dispersal of the vital energy leads to death. If life and death are closely related, then why should I worry about death?

143.【原文】凡物无成与毁，复通为一。 《庄子·齐物论》

【今译】一切事物从总体来看，没有完成和毁灭，都复归于一个整体。

【英译】For all the things in the world, there is no construction or destruction and everything belongs to a whole.

144.【原文】忘年忘义，振于无竟，故寓诸无竟。 《庄子·齐物论》

【今译】忘掉生死年岁，忘掉是非仁义，遨游于无穷的境地，这样圣人就把自己寄托于无穷无尽的境域之中了。

【英译】Forget about time, forget about justice, and travel in the realm of the infinite. Thus the sage can repose himself in the realm of the infinite.

145.【原文】因是已，已而不知其然，谓之道。 《庄子·齐物论》

【今译】顺着自然的规律走而不知道为什么这样，这就叫作道。

【英译】To follow the natural course of things without knowing why it is so is called Tao.

《荀子》
Xunzi

【简介】《荀子》成书于战国末年。它涉及范围极广，包括哲学、伦理、政治、经济、教育，乃至语言学、文学，是对当时百家思想和荀子自己学术思想的总结。荀子（约公元前313至公元前238年），名况，字卿，战国末期赵国人，著名思想家、文学家、政治家。荀子对儒家思想有所发展，提倡"性恶论"，强调后天环境和教育对人的影响，与孟子的"性善论"形成对比。

【Introduction】*Xunzi* written at the end of the Warring States period involves a wide range, including philosophy, ethics, politics, economy, education, linguistics and literature, which reveals Xunzi's ideology and other multiple ones from different schools in his age. With his family name Xun, given name Kuang, and alias Qing, Xunzi(c.313~238 BC) is a native of Zhao at the end of the Warring States period. As a famous thinker, writer and statesman, he developed Confucian school to some extent, and advocated "humans are bad in nature" which emphasizes the environmental and educational influence and which is a contrast of Mencius's view—"human are good in nature".

1. 【原文】相形不如论心，论心不如择术。形不胜心，心不胜术。　　《荀子·非相》

   【今译】观察形貌，不如评论人的思想；评论人的思想，不如考察他的行为。形貌不如思想说明问题，思想不如行为说明问题。

   【英译】Observing one person's facial expression is not so good as evaluating his thought; evaluating one person's thought is not so good as inspecting his behavior. The thought can show the question better than the facial expression. The behavior can show the question better than the thought.

2. 【原文】术正而心顺之，则形相虽恶而心术善，无害为君子也；形相虽善而心术恶，无害为小人也。　　《荀子·非相》

   【今译】行为端正而思想与行为一致，因此形象虽然丑陋而思想行为善良，不妨碍他成为君子；形貌虽然美好，而思想行为丑陋，也不妨碍他成为小人。

【英译】Behavior defines a person. If somebody is ugly in appearance and kind in mind, it does not prevent him from becoming a gentleman; if somebody is kind in appearance and ugly in mind, it does not prevent him from becoming an unprincipled person.

3. 【原文】人有三不祥：幼而不肯事长，贱而不肯事贵，不肖而不肯事贤。

《荀子·非相》

【今译】人有三种不祥的事情：年龄小的不肯侍奉年长的，地位低下的不肯侍奉地位高贵的，没有才能的不肯侍奉有才能的。

【英译】The person has three kinds of unpropitious matters: the young are not willing to serve the old, the person of low status is not willing to serve a person of noble status, and the person of no talent is not willing to serve a person of talent.

4. 【原文】天行有常，不为尧存，不为桀亡。应之以治则吉，应之以乱则凶。

《荀子·天论》

【今译】自然的运行是有正常规律的，并不因为偏爱尧而存在，也不因为厌恶桀而消失。以合理的行为来适应自然规律就吉利，以不合理的行为来扰乱自然规律就凶险。

【英译】The natural movement has its own normal rule. It exists certainly not because of Yao, nor does it vanish because of Jie. Adapting the natural law with the reasonable behavior is auspicious, while harassing the natural law with the irrational behavior is dangerous.

5. 【原文】强本而节用，则天不能贫；养备而动时，则天不能病；修道而不贰，则天不能祸。

《荀子·天论》

【今译】人类加强农业生产而节约用度，则上天也不能使其贫困；养生之道周备而行为适应天时，则上天也不能使其患病；遵循道义而没有偏差，则上天也不能加祸于他。

【英译】If the human beings strengthen the agricultural production and save the products, even the heaven cannot make us impoverished; if the way of life is complete and the conducts are in accordance with the weather, even the heaven cannot make us sick; if the human beings follow the morality and justice without any deviation, even the heaven cannot impose calamity on us.

6. 【原文】天有其时，地有其财，人有其治，夫是之谓能参。

《荀子·天论》

【今译】天有它的时节，地有它的财富，人有治理的能力，这就叫作能参豫天地。

【英译】The heaven has its seasons, the earth has its wealth, and the human beings have the ability of governing—this is called being concerned with the heaven and the earth.

7. 【原文】形具而神生，好恶、喜怒、哀乐臧焉，夫是之谓天情。　　《荀子·天论》

【今译】有了形体才有精神。所谓"天情"，是指人的精神活动是人的自然生理的功能，而人的喜怒哀乐自然生理也是天生的。

【英译】The human beings first have the shape then the spirit. The so-called "sentiment" refers to a person's spiritual activity and natural physiological function. A person's laughter, anger, sorrow, and happiness are also inborn.

8.【原文】天不为人之恶寒也辍冬，地不为人之恶辽远也辍广，君子不为小人之匈匈也辍行。 《荀子·天论》

【今译】天不会因为人们厌恶寒冷而废止冬季，大地不会因为人们厌恶路途遥远而缩小面积，君子不会因为小人气势汹汹叫嚷而改变自己的行为。

【英译】The heaven cannot abolish winter because the people loathe coldness. The earth cannot reduce the area because the people loathe the long journey. The gentleman cannot change his own behavior because of the villain's shouting.

9.【原文】故君子敬其在己者，而不慕其在天者；小人错其在己者，而慕其在天者。
《荀子·天论》

【今译】君子重视自身的修养努力，而不指望得到天的赐予；小人放弃自身的修养努力，而指望得到天的赐予。

【英译】The gentleman values his own efforts and does not count on the heaven's grant; the villain gives up his own efforts and counts on the heaven's grant.

10.【原文】在天者莫明于日月，在地者莫明于水火，在物者莫明于珠玉，在人者莫明于礼义。 《荀子·天论》

【今译】天上的事物没有比日月更明亮的了，地上的事物没有比水火更明亮的了，万物中没有比珠玉更明亮的了，人类社会中没有比懂得礼义的君子更明亮的了。

【英译】Nothing is so bright as the sun and the moon in the heaven; nothing is so bright as the water and fire on the earth; nothing is so bright as pearls and jade in the world; nobody is so bright as the gentleman who knows the rituals in the human society.

11.【原文】万物为道一偏，一物为万物一偏。愚者为一物一偏，而自以为知道，无知也。
《荀子·天论》

【今译】各种事物都只是道的一个方面，一种事物又只是各种事物的一个方面。愚蠢的人只了解一种事物的一个方面，可他还自以为认识了道，这实在是太无知了。

【英译】All the things are only one aspect of the way; one thing is one aspect of all things. The stupid person only understands one aspect of one thing, but he thinks he knows all. This is really the summit of ignorance.

12.【原文】君子居必择乡，游必就士，所以防邪辟而近中正也。 《荀子·劝学》

【今译】君子居住，一定选择风俗淳美的乡里；出外游学，一定选择有学问、有品行的贤士。这是为了防止邪辟、接近正直呀。

【英译】The gentleman certainly chooses the place of simplicity to live. The gentleman certainly chooses the virtuous and knowledgeable man to go with when he goes out to study. This is for preventing the evil and approaching the good.

13. **【原文】**材性知能，君子小人一也。好荣恶辱，好利恶害，是君子小人之所同也，若其所以求之之道则异矣。 《荀子·荣辱》

    【今译】才性和智能、君子和小人是一样的。爱好荣辱利益，厌恶耻辱危害，这也是君子和小人相同的地方，他们求取的方式却是不同的。

    【英译】The gentleman and the villain's natural disposition and intelligence are the same. The liking of benefit and loathing of shame are also the gentleman and the villain's common interests. Their ways of seeking are different.

14. **【原文】**凡人有所一同：饥而欲食，寒而欲暖，劳而欲息，好利而恶害，是人之所生而有也，是无待而然者也。 《荀子·荣辱》

    【今译】凡人都有同一的地方：饿了就想吃，冷了就盼望暖和，劳累了就要休息，喜欢利益而憎恶灾害，这是人生下来就有的品性，是无需外界影响就是如此的。

    【英译】The people all have the common interests. When a man is hungry, he wants to eat; when he feels cold, he hopes for the warm; when he is tired, he will rest. He likes the benefit but detests the disaster. This is the natural instinct not influenced by the outside.

15. **【原文】**人之生固小人，无师无法则唯利之见耳。 《荀子·荣辱》

    【今译】人一生下来，本来就是小人，不经过老师教育，不经过学习，就只看到利益。

    【英译】A man is born as a villain. If he is not cultivated by teachers and does not study, he can only see the benefit.

16. **【原文】**性也者，吾所不能为也，然而可化也。情也者，非吾所有也，然而可为也。 《荀子·儒效》

    【今译】本性，不是我们可以造作的，然而可以转化。积习，不是我们原本就具有的，但可以造作。

    【英译】The natural disposition is not what we can manufacture, but what we can transform. The habit is not what we have originally, but what we may get.

17. **【原文】**性者，天之就也；情者，性之质也；欲者，情之应也。以所欲为可得而求之，情之所必不免也；以为可而道之，知之所以出也。 《荀子·正名》

    【今译】本性是天生的。情感是本性的质体，欲望是情感的反映。把欲望的东西当作能得到的东西去追求，这是人的情感所不能避免的。以为可以得到，便去实行，这是人的智慧必然的选择。

【英译】The natural disposition is inborn. The emotion is its form and the desire is the reflection of emotion. Pursuing the desired thing as what can be obtained cannot be avoided by emotion. Implementing what can be obtained is the inevitable choice of wisdom.

18.【原文】人之性恶，其善者伪也。 《荀子·性恶》

【今译】人的本性是恶的，那善良是出于人为的。

【英译】The human natural disposition is wicked. That good behavior stems from one's intention.

19.【原文】今人之性恶，必将待师法然后正，得礼仪然后治。 《荀子·性恶》

【今译】今人的本性是恶的，一定要有师法的教化以后才能矫正，一定要有礼仪才能使社会得以治理。

【英译】The modern human natural instinct is evil. There must be enlightenment of instruction to rectify it, and there must be rituals to make the society well governed.

20.【原文】夫人虽有性质美而心辩知，必将求贤师而事之，择良友而友之。

《荀子·性恶》

【今译】一个人即使具有好的素质和辨别能力，也一定要跟着贤良的老师学习，选择好的朋友交往。

【英译】Even if one has the good quality and the ability to distinguish good from evil, he should also follow the virtuous teacher and make friends with the good.

21.【原文】学不可以已。 《荀子·劝学》

【今译】学习不能停止。

【英译】Study cannot stop.

22.【原文】木受绳则直，金就砺则利，君子博学而日参省乎己，则知明而行无过矣。

《荀子·劝学》

【今译】木材经墨线加工就变直了，刀剑在磨刀石上磨过就变得锋利了，君子广泛地学习而又能每天反省自己，那就会见识高明而行为无过错了。

【英译】The lumber becomes straight with the carpenter's ink thread; the sword becomes sharp after it is ground on the hone; the gentleman has great insights and conducts without mistakes, because he studies extensively and introspects himself every day.

23.【原文】吾尝终日而思矣，不如须臾之所学也；吾尝跂而望矣，不如登高之博见也。

《荀子·劝学》

【今译】我曾经整天地思考，但不及学习片刻所获得的教益。我曾经踮起脚跟瞭望，但比不上登上高处所见之广阔。

【英译】I used to ponder all day, but what I got was not so much as what I got in the study of a moment. I used to tiptoe to look, but what I could see was not so much as what I could see when I stood on the mountain.

24. 【原文】言有招祸也，行有招辱也，君子慎其所立乎！　　　　　　　　《荀子·劝学》

【今译】说话有时会招来灾祸，做事有时会招来耻辱，君子要谨慎地立身处世啊！

【英译】Speaking sometimes can incur disaster; working sometimes can incur shame. Therefore, the gentleman should get along with others cautiously in society.

25. 【原文】不积跬步，无以至千里；不积小流，无以成江海。　　　　　　《荀子·劝学》

【今译】不半步半步地积累，就无法到达千里之外；不汇集众多的小溪，就不能形成江海。

【英译】Without the accumulation of steps, we cannot cover the great distance; without the collection of the multitudinous rills, there will be no sea.

26. 【原文】君子之学也，入乎耳，箸乎心，布乎四体，行乎动静。端而言，蠕而动，一可以为法则。　　　　　　　　　　　　　　　　　　　　　　　　《荀子·劝学》

【今译】君子学习，要把所学到的东西听入耳中，牢记在心中，融会贯通到整个身心，并表现在举止行动上；哪怕是极细微的言行，都可以成为别人的榜样。

【英译】When the gentleman studies, he will listen to all he should study, keep them firmly in mind, comprehend them through the entire body and mind, and display them in all his conducts. All his words and deeds become others' example.

27. 【原文】礼恭而后可与言道之方，辞顺而后可与言道之理，色从而后可与言道之致。

《荀子·劝学》

【今译】来请教的人礼貌恭敬，然后才可以同他谈论道义的学习方法；言辞和顺，然后才可以和他谈论道义的原理；容色表现出乐于听从，然后才可以和他谈论道义的精深含义。

【英译】If the person who comes to consult is polite and respectful, I can discuss the study method with him; if he is obliging, I can discuss the principle of morality and justice with him; if he is glad to listen, then I may discuss the profound meaning of morality and justice with him.

28. 【原文】君子不傲、不隐、不瞽，谨顺其身。　　　　　　　　　　　　《荀子·劝学》

【今译】君子不急躁、不隐瞒、不盲目，谨慎地对待前来请教的人。

【英译】The gentleman is never irritable, concealing, nor blindfold, but treats the person who comes to consult cautiously.

29. 【原文】君子结于一也。 《荀子·劝学》

【今译】君子学习或办事总是专心致志。

【英译】The gentleman is always wholly absorbed when he studies and conducts business.

30. 【原文】志意修则骄富贵，道义重则轻王公，内省而外物轻矣。 《荀子·修身》

【今译】志向完美就能傲视权贵，看重道义就能鄙薄王公贵族，内心省察自己，就觉得外物轻微了。

【英译】If one's ambition is perfect, he can show disdain for the powerful officials; if he pays attention to morality and justice, he is able to despise the noble; if he consults his inner feelings, he will undervalue the external things.

31. 【原文】君子崇人之德，扬人之美，非谄谀也；正义直指，举人之过，非毁疵也。

《荀子·不苟》

【今译】君子尊崇别人的德行，宣扬别人的优点，不是谄媚阿谀别人；正义率直，指出别人的缺点，而不是故意诋毁别人。

【英译】The gentleman venerates others' morality and publicizes others' merits, which is not for flattering others; the gentleman points out others' shortcomings, which is not for slandering others intentionally.

32. 【原文】君子无爵而贵，无禄而富，不言而信，不怒而威，穷处而荣，独居而乐。

《荀子·儒效》

【今译】君子没有爵位也会高贵，没有俸禄也会富有，不用说话也能取信于人，不用发怒也有威严，处境贫困依然荣耀，处境孤独依然快乐。

【英译】Therefore, the gentleman can be noble without any title, wealthy without any official salary, trusted by others without speaking, dignified without getting angry, honored in poverty and happy in solitude.

33. 【原文】恭敬，礼也；调和，乐也；谨慎，利也；斗怒，害也。故君子安礼乐利，谨慎而无斗怒，是以百举而不过也。 《荀子·臣道》

【今译】恭敬，合乎礼节；协调和谐，合乎乐律；谨小慎微，则有好处；相互争斗，有害于人类。所以君子安守礼节，喜好音乐，言行谨慎，不互相争斗，因此一切行为都不会有过错。

【英译】Reverence should conform to rituals; harmony should conform to music; taking caution is beneficial and fighting is harmful. Therefore the gentlemen preserve the rituals, love music, take caution in their words and actions and avoid fighting. Thus, they are free of mistakes.

34. 【原文】明于天人之分，则可谓至人矣。 《荀子·天论》

【今译】明白天和人的区别，就可以叫作最高明的人了。

【英译】The person who knows the difference between the heaven and the human beings can be called the wisest.

35.【原文】君子敬始而慎终。终始如一，是君子之道、礼仪之文也。　　《荀子·礼论》

【今译】君子重视生，也慎重地对待死。始终如一，这就是君子的原则、礼义的仪式。

【英译】The gentleman values living as well as death constantly. This is the gentleman's principle and the ritual.

36.【原文】夫乐者，乐也，人之情所必不免也，故人不能无乐。乐则必发于声音，形于动静，而人之道，声音、动静、性术之变尽是矣。　　《荀子·乐论》

【今译】音乐，是娱乐，是人类情感不可避免的，所以人不能没有音乐。音乐必然抒发在声音上，表现在动静中，而人的声音、动静、性格行为的变化，都充分体现在这里了。

【英译】Music, a form of entertainment, is unavoidable by the human instinct. Therefore man cannot do without music. Music is inevitably expressed in sound and displayed in action. All the changes of sound, action and instinct are reflected in music.

37.【原文】君子耳不听淫声，目不视女色，口不出恶言，此三者，君子慎之。

《荀子·乐论》

【今译】君子耳朵不听淫靡的声音，眼睛不看女子的美貌，嘴不说恶言。这三种行为，君子要慎重。

【英译】Therefore, the gentleman turns a deaf ear to the extravagant sound, a blind eye to the beauty of girls, and never utters malicious words. The gentleman should be prudent in these three kinds of behaviors.

38.【原文】仁者之思也恭，圣人之思也乐，此治心之道也。　　《荀子·解蔽》

【今译】仁人的思想恭敬，圣人的思想快乐，这是修养身心的原则。

【英译】The kind person's thoughts are respectful and the sage's thoughts are joyful. This is the discipline of self-cultivation.

39.【原文】善学者尽其理，善行者究其难。　　《荀子·大略》

【今译】善于学习的人穷尽事物的道理，善于行动的人探究事物的难处。

【英译】The person who is good at studying seeks for the truth; the person who is good at taking actions probes into the difficulty.

40.【原文】岁不寒无以知松柏，事不难无以知君子。　　《荀子·大略》

【今译】年岁不寒冷，无法知道松柏的品性；事情不艰难，无法知道君子的素质才干。

【英译】The character of the pine and cypress shows in coldness and the gentleman's talent shows in hard times.

41. 【原文】小人不诚于内而求之于外。 《荀子·大略》

    【今译】小人不去加强内心的修养，而是追求外表。

    【英译】The villain never strengthens his own moral cultivation, but pursues the appearance.

42. 【原文】人之于文学也，犹玉之于琢磨也。 《荀子·大略》

    【今译】人学习文学，就好像玉必须琢磨一样。

    【英译】People study literature, just as the jade must be polished.

43. 【原文】学问不厌，好士不倦，是天府也。 《荀子·大略》

    【今译】勤学好问，不知满足；喜好儒士，不知疲倦，这是天然的知识宝库。

    【英译】Learn diligently and ask questions insatiably; make friends with Confucian scholars tirelessly. This is a natural repository.

44. 【原文】学者非必为仕，而仕者必如学。 《荀子·大略》

    【今译】学习不一定为了做官，而做官的人一定要好好学习。

    【英译】Study is not necessarily for an official post, but the officials must study hard.

45. 【原文】君人者不可以不慎取臣，匹夫不可以不慎取友。 《荀子·大略》

    【今译】君主不能不慎重地选择他的臣子，普通人不能不慎重地选择他的朋友。

    【英译】The monarch has to choose his official prudently; ordinary people have to choose friends prudently.

46. 【原文】多言而类，圣人也。少言而法，君子也。多言无法而流湎然，虽辩，小人也。

    《荀子·大略》

    【今译】说话多而符合礼义，这是圣人。说话少而符合法度，这是君子。说话多而不符合法度，滔滔不绝，虽然能言善辩，也是小人。

    【英译】The one who speaks much that is all in accordance with rituals is a sage. The one who speaks little that is all in accordance with the law is a gentleman. The one who speaks much that is not in accordance with the law, though reasonable, is a villain.

47. 【原文】芷兰生于深林，非以无人而不芳。 《荀子·宥坐》

    【今译】芷兰生长于深山老林，不因为没有人就不芳香。

    【英译】The orchids that grow in the deep forest will not give up the fragrance because there are no people.

48. 【原文】君子有三思，而不可不思也。少而不学，长无能也；老而不教，死无思也；有而不施，穷无与也。是故君子少思长，则学；老思死，则教；有思，穷则施也。

    《荀子·法行》

    【今译】君子有三个方面值得思索，而不可不思索。年少的时候不学习，长大就没有能力；年老的时候不教育别人，死后就没有人想念他；富有的时候不施舍，贫穷时就没有人接济他。所以君子年少时想着年老时就学习，年老时想着死后就教育别人，富有时想着穷困时就施舍。

【英译】The gentleman has three respects that are worth considering. If he does not study when he is young, he will have no ability after growing up; if he does not instruct others when he is old, he will not be missed by others after death; if he does not give alms when he is rich, he will not be given alms in poverty. So the gentleman studies thinking about getting old, instructs others thinking about death, gives alms thinking about poverty.

49.【原文】富贵不足以益也，卑贱不足以损也。如此，则可谓士矣。　　《荀子·哀公》

【今译】富贵不足以增益他，卑贱不足以损害他，这样就可以叫作士了。

【英译】If one cannot be benefited by wealth or harmed by poverty, he can be called a scholar.

50.【原文】君子贤而能容罢，知而能容愚，博而能容浅，粹而能容杂，夫是之谓兼术。

《荀子·非相》

【今译】君子有才能、德行而能容纳无能的人，聪明而能容纳愚昧的人，博学多闻而能容纳孤陋寡闻的人，品德纯洁而能容纳品行驳杂的人，这就叫作兼容并蓄的方法。

【英译】The gentleman is competent and can tolerate the incompetent people; the intelligent can tolerate the ignorant people; the well-informed can tolerate the ill-informed people; the pure in morality can tolerate the less pure people—this is called the way of toleration.

51.【原文】亲亲、故故、庸庸、劳劳，仁之杀也；贵贵、尊尊、贤贤、老老、长长，义之伦也。行之得其节，礼之序也。　　《荀子·大略》

【今译】亲近父母、不忘故交、论功行赏、按劳奖励，这是仁所表现的差别。尊重贵人、敬重贤者、敬奉老人、推崇长者，这是义所表现的伦理。实行起来适当，这就是礼的秩序。

【英译】Getting close to parents, not forgetting the old friends, and rewarding according to attribution—these are different reflections of benevolence. Respecting the noble, revering the virtuous, attending to the old, and praising the elders—these are reflections of morality. If it is properly implemented, it will be the order of the rituals.

52.【原文】青，取之于蓝，而青于蓝；冰，水为之，而寒于水。　　《荀子·劝学》

【今译】靛青是从蓼蓝中提取出来的，但颜色比蓼蓝更深；冰是水凝固而成的，但比水寒冷。

【英译】The color of indigo is derived from the indigo plant, but darker than the indigo plant; the ice is solidified from water, but colder than water.

53.【原文】不登高山，不知天之高也；不临深溪，不知地之厚也；不闻先王之遗言，不知学问之大也。　　　　　　　　　　　　　　　《荀子·劝学》

【今译】不登上高山，不知道天的高度；不亲临深溪，不知道大地的厚度；不聆听前代圣王的遗言，就不知道学问的渊博。

【英译】If one has never been to the top of a mountain, he does not know the height of the sky; if one has never been to be the deep stream, he does not know the thickness of the earth; if one does not listen to the words of the former king, he does not know the depth of the knowledge.

54.【原文】神莫大于化道，福莫长于无祸。　　　　　　　　　　　　《荀子·劝学》

【今译】精神修养没有比融于圣贤的道德更高的了，幸福没有比无灾无祸更长久的了。

【英译】There is nothing better than melting into the morals of sages for self-cultivation and there is nothing better than no trouble for happiness.

55.【原文】强自取柱，柔自取束。邪秽在身，怨之所构。　　　　　　《荀子·劝学》

【今译】坚强的东西自然被用作支柱，柔软的东西自然被用来捆束东西。邪恶污秽的东西存在于自身，是怨恨集结的原因。

【英译】The strong things are naturally used as the pillar; the soft things are naturally used for tying. The evil things existing in the person are the reason why the hatred concentrates.

56.【原文】声无小而不闻，行无隐而不形。　　　　　　　　　　　　《荀子·劝学》

【今译】声音无论怎样小，没有不被听到的；行为无论怎样隐蔽，没有不显露出来的。

【英译】No matter how little the sound is, it will be heard; no matter how concealing the behavior is, it will be known.

57.【原文】锲而舍之，朽木不折；锲而不舍，金石可镂。　　　　　　《荀子·劝学》

【今译】雕刻东西，如果半途放弃，即使是腐烂的木头也不能刻断；如果不停地刻下去，就连金属和石头都能镂空。

【英译】If we give up carving halfway, even the rotten log cannot be cut; if we carve ceaselessly, even the metal and stone can be engraved.

58.【原文】蓬生麻中，不扶而直；白沙在涅，与之俱黑。　　　　　　《荀子·劝学》

【今译】蓬草生在丛麻当中，不去扶植它也能挺直；白沙混入黑土中，会变得跟黑土一样黑。

【英译】Fluffy grass growing among hemp plants can be straight and upright; white sand mixed in the black earth will become black.

59.【原文】行衢道者不至，事两君者不容。目不能两视而明，耳不能两听而聪。

《荀子·劝学》

【今译】徘徊于歧路上的人不能到达目的地，同时侍奉两个君主的人在道义上不能相容。眼睛不同时看两件东西，就看得清楚；耳朵不同时听两种声音，就听得明白。

【英译】The person who is wandering up and down on the branch road can't reach the destination; the person who serves two kings at the same time can't be tolerated in morality and justice. Eyes cannot see two things clearly at the same time. Ears cannot hear two sounds clearly at the same time.

60. 【原文】无冥冥之志者，无昭昭之明；无惛惛之事者，无赫赫之功。　《荀子·劝学》

【今译】一个人要没有潜心钻研的精神，就不能明辨事理，洞察一切；不专心致志地工作，就不可能有显赫的成就。

【英译】If one has no concentrating spirit, he cannot understand the truth; if one does not work with single-heartedness, he cannot have illustrious achievements.

61. 【原文】君子洁其身，而同焉者合矣；善其言，而类焉者应矣。　《荀子·不苟》

【今译】君子洁修自身，同道的人就来会聚；修好自己的言论，同类的人就来呼应。

【英译】If the gentleman guides and corrects himself, people having a common goal will come to assemble; if the gentleman corrects his speech, people having a common goal will come to echo.

62. 【原文】见其可欲也，则必前后虑其可恶也者；见其可利也，则必前后虑其可害也者。

《荀子·不苟》

【今译】见到值得喜欢的一面，就一定要前前后后考虑它可厌的一面；见到有利的一面，就一定要前前后后考虑其有害的一面。

【英译】If we see one aspect of a thing that we like, we should consider its unattractive aspect; if we see one aspect of a thing that has interests, we should consider its harmful aspect.

63. 【原文】与人善言，煖于布帛；伤人之言，深于矛戟。　《荀子·荣辱》

【今译】和人说善良的话，让人比穿了棉衣还暖和；说伤人的话，比长矛刺人还厉害。

【英译】If we speak kind-heartedly, it can make people feel warmer than if they were dressed in cotton-padded clothes; if we speak scathingly, it hurts worse than the pike.

64. 【原文】自知者不怨人，知命者不怨天，怨人者穷，怨天者无志。失之己，反之人，岂不迂乎哉！　　《荀子·荣辱》

【今译】了解自己的人不埋怨别人，晓得自己命运的人不埋怨上天；埋怨别人的人会身陷困窘，埋怨上天的人没有志气。自己有了过失反而怪罪于他人，难道不是迂腐吗？

【英译】The person who understands himself does not blame others; the person who knows his own destiny does not blame the heaven. The person who blames others will get in trouble; the person who blames the heaven has no ambition. If he makes mistakes and puts the blame on others, isn't this stupid?

65.【原文】先义而后利者荣，先利而后义者辱。 《荀子·荣辱》

【今译】首先考虑道义而后考虑利益的人会得到荣誉，首先考虑利益而后考虑道义的人会受到屈辱。

【英译】The person who first considers morality and justice and then considers interests will get honor; the person who first considers interests and then considers morality and justice will get shame.

66.【原文】大巧在所不为，大智在所不虑。 《荀子·天论》

【今译】最能干的人在于懂得什么是不能做和不应做的，最聪明的人在于他不去考虑那些不能考虑和不应考虑的事。

【英译】The most competent person understands what cannot be done and should not be done; the cleverest person does not consider the thing that he is unable to consider and should not consider.

67.【原文】无用吾之所短遇人之所长。 《荀子·大略》

【今译】不要用自己的短处去对付别人的长处。

【英译】Never deal with others' strong point with one's own weakness.

68.【原文】雨小，汉故潜。 《荀子·大略》

【今译】雨虽然下得小，但仍能深深地渗入地下。

【英译】The tender rain can permeate underground deeply.

69.【原文】凡物有乘而来，乘其出者，是其反者也。 《荀子·大略》

【今译】大凡事物的出现，都有原因。人们行动的后果，原因都在自己以往的所作所为。

【英译】All the happenings have their reasons. The consequences of one man's actions all lie in what he has done.

70.【原文】不知其子视其友，不知其君视其左右。 《荀子·性恶》

【今译】不了解他的儿子，看看他儿子的朋友就清楚了；不了解君主，看看君主左右的近臣就清楚了。

【英译】If you do not know the son, see his son's friends; if you do not know the ruler, see his officials.

71.【原文】天之所覆，地之所载，莫不尽其美。 《荀子·王制》

【今译】苍天覆盖的一切，大地负载的一切，没有一样东西不竭尽它们的美妙。

【英译】All things that the sky covers and the earth loads can express their wonders.

72. 【原文】乱则国危，治则国安。 　　　　　　　　　　　　　　　《荀子·王霸》

    【今译】社会混乱，国家就危殆；社会治平，国家就安定。

    【英译】If the society is in disorder, the country will be in great danger; if the society is well governed, the country will be stable.

73. 【原文】能当一人而天下取，失当一人而社稷危。 　　　　　　　《荀子·王霸》

    【今译】能恰当地任用一个人就可以取得天下，不能恰当地任用一个人国家就会危殆。

    【英译】If one can appoint people appropriately, he can conquer the world; if one cannot appoint people appropriately, the country will be in great danger.

74. 【原文】主道治近不治远，治明不治幽，治一不治二。 　　　　　《荀子·王霸》

    【今译】君主治理国家的办法是治理近处的事，不治理远处的事；治理明显的事，不治理没出现的事；治理主要的事，不治理繁杂的事。

    【英译】The key to managing the country is to deal with the immediate things instead of the remote things, to deal with the explicit things instead of the implicit things, to deal with the major things instead of the minor things.

75. 【原文】用国者，得百姓之力者富，得百姓之死者强，得百姓之誉者荣。

    　　　　　　　　　　　　　　　　　　　　　　　　　　　　《荀子·王霸》

    【今译】治理国家的人，能得到百姓尽力的就能使国家富有，能得到百姓为他拼死而战的就能使国家强盛，能得到百姓的称颂就能使自身有名望。

    【英译】The ruler with the help of the people can make the country rich; the ruler with the people's loyalty can make the country powerful; the ruler with the praise of the people can make himself prestigious.

76. 【原文】法者，治之端也；君子者，法之原也。 　　　　　　　　《荀子·君道》

    【今译】法制，是治理国家的根本；君子，则是实行法制的根本。

    【英译】The legal system is the fundament of managing the country; the gentleman is the fundament of implementing the legal system.

77. 【原文】川渊深而鱼鳖归之，山林茂而禽兽归之，邢政平而百姓归之，礼义备而君子归之。 　　　　　　　　　　　　　　　　　　　　　　　　《荀子·致士》

    【今译】河深渊深，鱼鳖就会归向它；山林茂密，禽兽就会归向它；刑法政治公平，百姓就会归向它；礼仪完备，君子就会归向它。

    【英译】If the river and abyss are deep, fish and turtles will swim to them; if the mountain forest is prosperous, the birds and beasts will come to it; if the law and the politics are fair, the people will submit to them; if the etiquette is complete, the gentleman will turn to it.

78. 【原文】不富无以养民情，不教无以理民性。 　　　　　　　　　《荀子·大略》

【今译】不富，就不能培养百姓的性情；不教诲，就不能理顺百姓的本性。

【英译】Without wealth, the king cannot cultivate the people's emotion; without teaching, the king cannot rectify the people's natural instinct.

79. 【原文】人无礼则不生，事无礼则不成，国家无礼则不宁。　　　　《荀子·修身》

【今译】人没有礼仪就不能生存，做事情没有礼仪就办不成，国家没有礼仪就不安宁。

【英译】Without ritual, the people cannot live, things cannot be done, and the country will not be stable.

《吕氏春秋》
The Spring and Autumn of Lü Buwei

【简介】《吕氏春秋》是中国历史上第一部有组织、按计划编写的文集，大约在公元前239年完成。《吕氏春秋》内容丰富，涉及面广，除包括天文、地理、阴阳、五行、气候、音乐、教育、军事、养生等，还记载了大量的历史资料。《吕氏春秋》是由秦国丞相吕不韦（约公元前292年至公元前235年）召集其门客编撰而成。吕不韦原是商人，他为人慷慨，广泛结交士人，门客多达3 000人。

【Introduction】*The Spring and Autumn of Lü Buwei* is the first anthology in Chinese history which was compiled by an organized group with its compiling plans. It was done in about c.239 BC. It has a rich content which includes astronomy, geography, the thoughts of Yin and Yang, Wuxing, climate, music, education, military and regimen and so on, and it also contains a large amount of historical materials. It was written by Lü Buwei's guests. Lü Buwei(c.?~235 BC), a former merchant, became the prime minister of the state of Qin. He consorted plenty of intellectuals and treated them so friendly and generously that his guests reached up to 3 000 at a time.

1. 【原文】东风解冻，蛰虫始振。鱼上冰，獭祭鱼。候雁北。　　　　《吕氏春秋·孟春》

【今译】春风吹拂，冰雪消融，蛰伏的动物开始苏醒并且活动起来。鱼儿从深水向上游到冰层下，水獭开始捕鱼，大雁北飞。

【英译】The spring wind thaws the frozen surface of the earth. All dormant animals and insects begin to come to life again. Fishes start to come to the surface of the icy water. Otters start to catch fish. Migrant wild geese fly north.

2. 【原文】始生之者天也，养成之者人也。 《吕氏春秋·本生》

【今译】最初创造生命的，是天；养育生命并使它成长的，是人。

【英译】Everything in the world is created by heaven, then raised by human beings.

3. 【原文】夫水之性清，土者抇之，故不得清。人之性寿，物者抇之，故不得寿。 《吕氏春秋·本生》

【今译】水的本性是清澈的，由于泥土使它变得混浊，所以不能保持清澈。人的天性是能够长寿的，由于有外物干扰它，所以不能长寿。

【英译】According to the nature of water, it is crystal-clear. Nevertheless, it cannot be clear while earth is poured into it. According to human nature, man can enjoy a long lifespan. Nevertheless, longevity is not possible because life is disturbed with too many external factors.

4. 【原文】天生人而使有贪有欲。欲有情，情有节，圣人修节以止欲，故不过行其情也。故耳之欲五声，目之欲五色，口之欲五味，情也。 《吕氏春秋·情欲》

【今译】天创造了人并且使他们有贪心，有欲望。欲望产生情欲，情欲应该有所节制。圣人节制自己来克制欲望，所以不会放纵情欲。耳朵想听各种优美的声音，眼睛想看各种美丽的色彩，嘴巴想吃各种美味的食物，这都是情欲。

【英译】Human beings are created by heaven and they are born with desires and lusts. Desires lead to lusts, and lusts should be constrained. Sages take control over their own lives and restrain their lusts, so they are not overly addicted to them. It is natural that the ear loves all the five euphonious notes, the eye loves all the five beautiful colours, the mouth loves al the five savoury tastes, and these cases can be regarded as a form of lust.

5. 【原文】耳不乐声，目不乐色，口不甘味，与死无择。 《吕氏春秋·情欲》

【今译】耳朵听着优美的声音也不觉得快乐，眼睛看着美丽的色彩也不觉得高兴，嘴里吃着美味的食物却不觉得香甜，这实际上跟死没有什么区别。

【英译】After they get into trouble, they will not feel pleased even when they are listening to wonderful tunes, will not feel happy even when they are appreciating the most beautiful colours, nor will they feel satisfied even when they are eating the most delicious food. Even though they are alive, they can be considered as nothing but walking corpses.

6. 【原文】秋早寒则冬必暖矣，春多雨则夏必旱矣。 《吕氏春秋·情欲》

【今译】秋天冷得过早，冬天就必定会温暖；春天多雨，夏天就必定会干旱。

【英译】If cold weather comes early in autumn, it will be followed by a warm winter. If it rains frequently in spring, it will be followed by a dry summer.

7. 【原文】万物之形虽异，其情一体也。　　　　　　　　　　　　《吕氏春秋·情欲》

   【今译】虽然万物的形状千差万别，但它们的本性都是一样的。

   【英译】Even though tens of thousands of things in the world have various shapes, they all have the same inbeing.

8. 【原文】由其道，功名之不可得逃，犹表之与影，若呼之与响。　《吕氏春秋·功名》

   【今译】遵循正道，功名就一定无法逃脱，如同影子跟随着竖起的木表，回音跟随着呼声一样。

   【英译】If all actions are taken in the right way, one is destined to be successful and famous. That is as natural as shadows following objects and echoes responding to shouting.

9. 【原文】水泉深则鱼鳖归之，树木盛则飞鸟归之，庶草茂则禽兽归之，人主贤则豪杰归之。故圣王不务归之者，而务其所以归。　　　　　《吕氏春秋·功名》

   【今译】水深之处，鱼鳖就会聚集到那里；树木繁盛，飞鸟就会聚集到那里；百草茂密，禽兽就会聚集到那里；君主贤明，豪杰就会归附于他。所以，圣明的君主并不致力于使人们归依自己，而是致力于修养自己的德行。

   【英译】If waters and springs are deep, fishes and turtles will gather there. If trees are resplendent, birds will gather there. If grasses are lush in an area, wild animals will gather there. And if the sovereign is sensible and outstanding, people will gather around him. Therefore, sage sovereigns do not pay much attention to submitting people, but are concerned with cultivating their virtues.

10. 【原文】强令之笑不乐，强令之哭不悲。强令之为道也，可以成小，而不可以成大。

    《吕氏春秋·功名》

    【今译】勉强做出来的笑并不真的快乐，勉强做出来的哭并不真的悲哀。勉强做事，只能做成一些小事，而不可能成就大业。

    【英译】If one is forced to laugh, he will not feel happy in the heart. If one is forced to cry, he will not feel sad in the heart. If one is forced to do something, he can only achieve some small goals. However, it is not possible for him to reach outstanding ones.

11. 【原文】欲取天下，天下不可取；可取，身将先取。　　　　　《吕氏春秋·先己》

    【今译】一心只想治理好天下，天下也不可能治理好。如果要治理好天下，首先要修养自己的心性。

    【英译】The world cannot be put in order even though you are committed to that goal. And if you really want to put the world in order, the thing you should start with is to cultivate your mind.

12. 【原文】昔者先圣王成其身而天下成，治其身而天下治。 《吕氏春秋·先己》

   【今译】古代圣明的帝王进行自我修养，能够修养自身，就能够治理天下；自身修养好了，天下也就治理好了。

   【英译】Sage sovereigns of ancient times were committed to cultivating their minds. They were able to govern the world since they were able to cultivate their own minds, and when their minds were well cultivated, the world was put in order as well.

13. 【原文】善响者不于响，于声；善影者不于影，于形；为天下者不于天下，于身。

   《吕氏春秋·先己》

   【今译】擅长发声的人，不致力于回声，而致力于改善自己的声音；擅长改善影子的人，不致力于影子，而致力于改善客观的形体；治理天下的人，不要致力于天下，而要致力于自我修养。

   【英译】Whoever is good at making sounds will concentrate on improving the sound source instead of the resonance. Whoever is good at making images will concentrate on designing substantial figures instead of paying too much attention to the shadows. And whoever is good at governing the world will concentrate on cultivating his mind instead of paying too much attention to the world.

14. 【原文】顺性则聪明寿长，平静则业进乐乡。 《吕氏春秋·先己》

   【今译】顺应生命的天性就能够聪明而且长寿；平和清净就会事业发展，百姓乐于归化。

   【英译】If he is in accordance with the nature of life, he will become wiser and can also enjoy longevity. If he remains even-tempered, his undertakings can be done well, moreover, common people will be ready to submit to his authority.

15. 【原文】欲胜人者必先自胜，欲论人者必先自论，欲知人者必先自知。

   《吕氏春秋·先己》

   【今译】想要战胜别人，首先要战胜自己；想要评判别人，首先要评判自己；想要了解别人，首先要了解自己。

   【英译】Anyone who wants to surmount others should surmount himself first; anyone who wants to point out the shortcomings of others should know his own shortcomings first; anyone who wants to know others should know himself first.

16. 【原文】先王之教，莫荣于孝，莫显于忠。 《吕氏春秋·劝学》

   【今译】按照先王的教导，没有什么比孝更荣耀的，没有什么比忠更尊显的。

   【英译】According to ancient kings, nothing is more honourable than complying with the principle of filial piety and nothing is more respectable than loyalty.

17. 【原文】师之教也，不争轻重尊卑贫富而争于道。　　　　　　　　　《吕氏春秋·劝学》

    【今译】老师施教的时候，也不计较学生的轻重、尊卑、贫富，而是看重他是否能够接受理义。

    【英译】As for the teachers, they should not pay any attention to factors such as whether their pupils are powerful or powerless, rich or poor, whether they come from a family with noble background or from a common family. The only thing that should matter to the teachers is whether their pupils are really capable of mastering what they are to be taught.

18. 【原文】凡说者，兑之也，非说之也。　　　　　　　　　　　　　　《吕氏春秋·劝学》

    【今译】凡是施教，都要循循善诱地进行教诲，而不是要取悦对方。

    【英译】Regarding the education of others, the teacher should practise in a correct, interesting manner so that his teachings will be accepted and remembered by the pupils, instead of endearing himself to them and catering to their interests.

19. 【原文】师必胜理行义然后尊。　　　　　　　　　　　　　　　　　《吕氏春秋·劝学》

    【今译】老师一定要依循事理，施行道义，然后才能受到尊敬。

    【英译】A teacher can be respected and honoured only when he adheres to the fixed principles and practises morality and justice in person.

20. 【原文】凡学，非能益也，达天性也。　　　　　　　　　　　　　　《吕氏春秋·尊师》

    【今译】学习并不能给人增添什么，而只是使人通晓天性。

    【英译】Learning is not a way to gain talents. On the contrary, it is a way for human beings to master the innate nature of life.

21. 【原文】故教也者，义之大者也；学也者，知之盛者也。　　　　　　《吕氏春秋·尊师》

    【今译】施教是一件非常仁义的举动，学习是一件非常睿智的事情。

    【英译】Teaching is the most benevolent profession and study is the most important measure for disseminating morality and justice.

22. 【原文】知之盛者莫大于成身，成身莫大于学。　　　　　　　　　　《吕氏春秋·尊师》

    【今译】在所有睿智的事情中，再没有比修养身心更大的了；而在修养身心中，再没有什么比学习更重要的了。

    【英译】Among all wise activities, nothing could be more meaningful than cultivating one's mind, and in cultivating one's mind, nothing could be more important than learning.

23. 【原文】人之情不能乐其所不安，不能得于其所不乐。　　　　　　　《吕氏春秋·诬徒》

    【今译】按照人之常情，人们不能从使自己感到不安的事物中得到快乐，不能从使自己不快乐的事物中有所收获。

【英译】According to human nature, they will not be pleased with things which threaten them, nor can they learn anything from things in which they have no interest.

24.【原文】物固莫不有长，莫不有短。人亦然故善学者假人之长以补其短。

《吕氏春秋·用众》

【今译】事物本来都有各自的长处与短处。人也是这样的。所以善于学习的人，能借鉴别人的长处来弥补自己的短处。

【英译】Everything in the world has both weak points and strong points. Human beings are the same. Therefore, those who are really good at learning will overcome their own weak points by learning from the strong points of others.

25.【原文】夫取于众，此三皇五帝之所以大立功名也。 《吕氏春秋·用众》

【今译】博采众人的长处，所以三皇五帝才得以建立高功盛名。

【英译】Therefore, the Three Sovereigns and Five Emperors accomplished magnificent achievements and gained great reputations by making good use of each person's strong points.

26.【原文】四时代兴，或暑或寒，或短或长，或柔或刚。 《吕氏春秋·大乐》

【今译】春夏秋冬交替出现，四季有寒有暑，白昼有长有短，万物有刚有柔。

【英译】The four seasons take their turns to come. Sometimes it is cold, but at other times it is hot. Sometimes the day is long, but at other times it is short. Some things are soft but others are hard.

27.【原文】声出于和，和出于适。 《吕氏春秋·大乐》

【今译】声音产生于和谐，和谐来自于适度。

【英译】The sound can be euphonious only when it is harmonious, and euphony can be created only when it is moderate.

28.【原文】凡乐，天地之和，阴阳之调也。 《吕氏春秋·大乐》

【今译】大凡音乐，都是天地和谐、阴阳调和的产物。

【英译】Music is based on the harmonious relationship between heaven and earth, between Yin and Yang.

29.【原文】道也者，至精也，不可为形，不可为名，强为之，谓之太一。

《吕氏春秋·大乐》

【今译】道是最为精妙的，不能描绘它的形状，也不能给它命名，如果要勉强给它起个名字，就把它叫作"太一"。

【英译】Tao is the subtlest thing. No one can describe its shape or address it by name. If a name must be given, call it "Tai Yi" (or the Great One).

30.【原文】人莫不以其生生，而不知其所以生；人莫不以其知知，而不知其所以知。

《吕氏春秋·侈乐》

【今译】人无不因为自己有生命而生存，但却不知道自己为什么会有生命；人无不因为自己有智慧而可以认知，但却不知道自己为什么会有智慧。

【英译】People of the world live because they are conferred life. However, no one knows why he is conferred life. They can know things because each of them is conferred intelligence. However, no one knows why he is conferred intelligence.

31.【原文】凡古圣王之所为贵乐者，为其乐也。　　　　　　　《吕氏春秋·侈乐》

【今译】古代圣明的帝王之所以重视音乐，是因为它能使人快乐。

【英译】The reason why sensible and wise sovereigns of ancient times pay so much attention to music is that music can make people feel happy.

32.【原文】乐之有情，譬之若肌肤形体之有情，性也。有情性则必有性养矣。

《吕氏春秋·侈乐》

【今译】音乐有真谛，如同肌肤身体有情性一样，有情性就必须要进行颐养。

【英译】Music has soul rather the same as a human being does—every people possesses not only a body but a disposition, so one should always take good care of himself.

33.【原文】遂而不返，制乎嗜欲。制乎嗜欲无穷，则必失其天矣。　《吕氏春秋·侈乐》

【今译】一味沉溺于外物而不返回生命的天性，就会被嗜欲所制约；追求无穷的嗜欲就必定会丧失生命的天性。

【英译】If they are too addicted to external factors and overlook the true nature of life, they will be enslaved by their own wishes and lusts and as a result, the nature of life will become totally lost.

34.【原文】欲之者耳目鼻口也，乐之弗乐者心也。心必和平然后乐。

《吕氏春秋·适音》

【今译】有各种欲望的，是耳、目、鼻、口；而决定快乐不快乐的，是心。心必须平和，然后才能快乐。

【英译】Ear, eye, nose and mouth are organs with desires constantly seeking satisfaction. However, the heart is the decisive factor in making one happy or unhappy. One can feel happy only when the heart is tranquil and peaceful.

35.【原文】乐之务在于和心，和心在于行适。　　　　　　　　《吕氏春秋·适音》

【今译】快乐的关键在于使内心平和，内心平和的关键在于行止得当。

【英译】It is of prime importance to remain tranquil and peaceful in the heart. And the most important thing in realizing that is to behave correctly and decently.

36.【原文】夫乐有适，心亦有适。　　　　　　　　　　　　《吕氏春秋·适音》

【今译】音乐要适中，心也要适中。

【英译】Music should be moderate, and the heart of human being should be moderate as well.

37.【原文】人之情欲寿而恶夭，欲安而恶危，欲荣而恶辱，欲逸而恶劳。

《吕氏春秋·适音》

【今译】按照人之常情，人们希望长寿而讨厌短命，希望安全而讨厌危险，希望荣耀而讨厌蒙受耻辱，希望安逸而讨厌劳顿。

【英译】According to the nature of human beings, everyone wishes to enjoy longevity and hopes to avoid dying young. They wish to be safe and avoid threat. They wish to be honoured and hate humiliation. They wish to lead comfortable and idyllic lives and hate being burdened with hard tasks.

38.【原文】胜理以治国则法立，法立则天下服矣。　　　《吕氏春秋·适音》

【今译】遵循事理来治理国家，法度就能够确立；法度确立了，天下人就会服从。

【英译】If a sovereign governs his state according to these rules and principles, the law will be well established. When the law is well established, people of the world will submit to his authority.

39.【原文】众正之所积，其福无不及也；众邪之所积，其祸无不逮也。

《吕氏春秋·明理》

【今译】诸多正义积聚的地方，幸福就会降临；诸多邪气积聚的地方，灾祸就会临头。

【英译】Good fortunes will come if righteousness surrounds you; misfortunes will occur if devils congregate around you.

参考文献
Bibliography

1. Myles Smith. *The Translators to the Reader: Holy Bible*. London: Trinitarian Bible Society, 2007.

2. 蔡希勤. 管子说：汉英对照. 北京：华语教学出版社，2011.

3. [春秋] 孔丘. 论语选萃. 付雅丽译. 北京：中国对外翻译出版公司，2010.

4. 王恒展，杨敏. 庄子语录：汉英双语版. 济南：山东友谊出版社，2011.

5. [春秋] 老子. 老子的智慧：汉英对照（上、下册）. 林语堂英译. 合肥：安徽科学技术出版社，2012.

6. 刘希茹，李照国. 黄帝内经·素问（Ⅰ、Ⅱ、Ⅲ）. 西安：世界图书出版西安公司，2008.

7. 刘希茹，李照国. 黄帝内经·灵枢（Ⅰ、Ⅱ、Ⅲ）. 西安：世界图书出版西安公司，2005.

8. 刘毓庆，李蹊. 诗经. 北京：中华书局，2011.

9. 钱钟书. 管锥编. 北京：中华书局，1979.

10. 汪榕培，潘智丹. 英译《诗经·国风》. 上海：上海外语教育出版社，2008.

11. [战国] 墨翟. 墨子（Ⅰ、Ⅱ）. 周才珠，齐瑞端今译，汪榕培，王宏英译. 长沙：湖南人民出版社，2006.

12. 王恒展，杨敏. 荀子语录：汉英双语版. 济南：山东友谊出版社，2011.

13. 杨伯峻，赵甄陶等. 孟子：汉英对照. 长沙：湖南人民出版社，1999.

14. [意] 伊塔洛·卡尔维诺. 为什么读经典. 黄灿然，李桂蜜译. 南京：译林出版社，2012.

15. 翟江月. 吕氏春秋. 桂林：广西师范大学出版社，2005.

16. 张华松. 道德经：汉英双语版. 合肥：安徽人民出版社，2012.

17. 肖川. 什么是良好的教育. 基础教育课程，2014（18）.

18. Junfang Sun. *Medical Implication in the Bible and Its Relevance to Modern Medicine*. Journal of Integrative Medicine, 2013(06).

后 记

书在结稿付梓之时,那些美丽的、充满着古老智慧的诗词依然如袅袅余音在脑海中徘徊不去。

科技在发展,整个社会因科技的进步而受益。然而,如果人们错误地认为新事物一定优越于旧事物,那么这种"新"必然会带来破坏。因为智慧并非一定随着时光的流逝而增长,在很多主要的科技领域,无数的探索所揭示的新发现实际上只是一些古老知识的再发现而已。

因此,明智的做法是,我们既要学习现代化的新知识,又要常常温习传统的古老智慧,这对我们的身心发展都是不无裨益的。

难忘那些捧书在手、字斟句酌的不眠之夜,难忘那些逐字校对、反复审核的艰辛。我们将此作品归功于所有支持该项目的人,以及那些在幕后默默付出的朋友和家人。这是一项多人合作的项目,但同时也有必要指明其间的分工:本书的主要选题和策划由孙俊芳老师负责,她还编写了书中第1章到第3章;李晓婧老师负责编写第4章到第7章第1部分;李蕊老师负责编写第7章第2部分到第10章。郭先英老师负责全书的审核、校对和专业指导,并对所选句段的译本进行甄别和选择。

也借此机会特别鸣谢为这本书提供了宝贵资源的文献,本书选材的今译和英译部分主要参考了下列文献:刘毓庆、李蹊的《诗经》(2011),汪榕培、潘智丹的《英译〈诗经·国风〉》(2008),刘希茹、李照国的《黄帝内经·灵枢》(2008)和《黄帝内经·素问》(2005),林语堂英译的《老子的智慧:汉英对照》(上下册)(2012),蔡希勤的《管子说》(2011),付雅丽英译的《论语选萃》(2010),周才珠、齐瑞端、汪榕培、王宏的《墨子》(2006),杨伯峻、赵甄陶等的《孟子》(1999),王恒展、杨敏的《庄子语录:汉英双语版》(2011)和《荀子语录:汉英双语版》(2011),翟江月的《吕氏春秋》(2005)。没有这些宝贵的资源,这本书就不可能成形。

需要说明的是,由于人们对于这些古老的句子有不同的理解,个别地方今译和英译不完全一致,也希望此书出版之后能听到读者反馈宝贵的意见。

我们盼望这本书的早日面世,如同盼望一个新生儿的出生。但愿这本书能带着岁月的馨香,带领我们走进锦绣般的诗词,走进古老的智慧,走进永远的历史……

Epilogue

It's time to finish the work and submit it to publication, but the beautiful words and sentences and the ancient wisdom in them are still lingering in my heart.

As technology progresses, the whole society benefits from the advance, yet the newness sometimes brings damage due to the misconception that the new is inherently better than the old. Yet, wisdom is not bound by the flow of calendar. And many researches reveal that modern discoveries are actually a rediscovery of ancient knowledge practically in all major fields of technology and sciences.[①]

So it's wise to study both the tradition and the knowledge of modern world in our quest to benefit our body and soul.

It's hard to forget all those sleepless nights with books in hands, chewing on the classic words and sentences; and hard to forget those word-by-word proofreading and double-checking with the original copies. We attribute this piece of work to all those who support our program and those who are helping us behind the scene. It's a wonderful cooperation among four people but it's also necessary to point out the division of the work. Ms. Sun Junfang selects the theme and devises the whole program. She is also in charge of Part One to Part Three; Li Xiaojing is in charge of Part Four to the first section of Part Seven; Li Rui is in charge of the second section of Part Seven to Part Ten. Guo Xianying is in charge of the supervision, proofreading and professional guidance of the program. She also contributes to the selecting of the translations.

We would like to take this opportunity to extend our great thanks to the books which provide us with valuable resources. We refer to the following works for our translation part: *The Book of Poetry*(2011) by Liu Yuqing and Li Xi, *Regional Songs from The Book of Poetry*(2008) by Wang Rongpei, Pan Zhidan, *Yellow Emperor's Canon of Medicine • Spiritual Pivot*(2008) and *Yellow Emperor's Canon of Medicine • Plain Conversation*(2005) by Liu

---

① Junfang Sun. *Medical Implication in the Bible and Its Relevance to Modern Medicine*. Journal of Integrative Medicine. 2013（06）.

Xiru and Li Zhaoguo, *The Wisdom of Laotse*(I、II)(2012) translated by Lin Yutang, *Guanzi Says*(2012) by Cai Xiqin, *Quotations from The Analects of Confucius*(2010) by Fu Yali, *Mozi*(2006) by Zhou Caizhu, Qi Ruiduan, Wang Rongpei and Wang Hong, *Mencius*(1999) by Yang Bojun, Zhao Zhentao, etc., *Quotations from Zhuangzi*(2011) and *Quotations from Xunzi*(2011) by Wang Hengzhan and Yangmin, *The Spring and Autumn of Lü Buwei*(2005) by Zhai Jiangyue. Without these resources, the publication of this book will be impossible.

Another thing to point out is that since people have different interpretations to the ancient sayings, some modern versions do not quite accord with the English translation. We hope to get some feedback about this from the readers after the publication of the book.

We are anxiously looking forward to the debut of the book, just like looking forward to the birth of a new baby. We hope this book, with the fragrance of years, can lead us into the charm of the poems, the ancient wisdom, and the history forever…